PENGUIN VEER

THE BATTLE OF HAJI PIR

A product of the Naval Officers' Academy, Kulpreet Yadav spent two decades as an officer in uniform and successfully commanded three ships in his career. Since his retirement as commandant from the Indian Coast Guard in 2014, he has authored several books in diverse genres, including military history, espionage and true crime. Kulpreet's previous book, titled *Brahmaputra*, was co-written with Vijayendra Prasad, the screenwriter of blockbuster films like *Baahubali*, *RRR* and *Bajrangi Bhaijaan*, among others. His military history book, *The Battle of Rezang La*, was released in 2021. Kulpreet is also an actor, a film-maker and an entrepreneur.

PENGUIN VEER

Penguin Veer is an imprint of the Penguin Random House group of companies whose addresses can be found at global.penguinrandomhouse.com

Published by Penguin Random House India Pvt. Ltd
4th Floor, Capital Tower 1, MG Road,
Gurugram 122 002, Haryana, India

Penguin
Random House
India

First published in Penguin Veer by Penguin Random House India 2024

10 9 8 7 6 5 4 3 2 1

This book is a work of non-fiction. The views and opinions expressed in the book are those of the author only and do not reflect or represent the views and opinions held by any other person. This book is based on a variety of sources, including published materials and research conducted by the author, and on interviews and interactions of the author with the persons mentioned in the manuscript. It reflects the author's own understanding and conception of such materials and/or can be verified by research. All persons within the book are actual individuals and the names and characteristics of some individuals have been changed to respect their privacy. The objective of this book is not to hurt any sentiments or be biased in favour of or against any particular person, political party, region, caste, society, gender, creed, nation or religion.

Please note that no part of this book may be used or reproduced in any manner for the purpose of training artificial intelligence technologies or systems.

ISBN 9780143469254

Typeset in Adobe Garamond Pro by Manipal Technologies Limited, Manipal
Printed at Thomson Press India Ltd, New Delhi

www.penguin.co.in

MIX
Paper | Supporting
responsible forestry
FSC® C010615

THE BATTLE OF HAJI PIR

THE INDIAN ARMY'S CROSS-BORDER SURGICAL STRIKE

KULPREET YADAV

PENGUIN
VEER

An imprint of Penguin Random House

The names of people, places and events in this book are true. However, to aid comprehension for non-Army readers, certain scenes in a few places have been recreated with the help of dialogue. These dialogues have been reconstructed based on factual accounts present in the public domain, available official records of the battle, personal interviews and logical suppositions arrived at based on these.

'*The Battle of Haji Pir was a prestigious operation and the Indian troops spared no effort to make it a great success. It was well-planned and skilfully executed. The courage and determination of the commanders as well as the high morale of the troops ensured its success. There were many heroes in the Battle of Haji Pir, but the one who stood tall above all was Major Ranjit Singh Dyal, who led the assault on Sank and captured the most valuable and terminal objective of Haji Pir Pass.*'

—Lt Gen. P.C. Katoch, PVSM, UYSM, AVSM, SC (retd)

'*1 Para's capture of Haji Pir, followed by the impressive takeover of the entire bulge by 68 and 93 Brigades, showcased the bravery of Indian Army officers and jawans. Battling adverse weather and rugged mountain terrain, the Indian Army triumphed against heavy odds, attributing their success to superior training, unwavering fitness and a determined attitude.*'

—Lt Gen. M.A. Gurbaxani, PVSM, AVSM (retd)

'*Captured by a bold and unorthodox operation against all odds and in inclement weather, Haji Pir was the only 1965 Indo–Pak war operation which India had successfully concluded from start to end.*'

—Maj. Gen. Raj Mehta, AVSM, VSM (retd)

'The capture of the Haji Pir Pass was the most successful operation of the 1965 war. Major Ranjit Singh Dyal of 1 Para (later Army Commander, Southern Command) captured Sank despite heavy rain, and swiftly moved on to Sar and Ledwali Gali. His troops climbed 1200 metres at night and captured the Haji Pir Pass by 28 August 1965. This unnerved the higher echelons of the Pakistan Army.'

—Maj. Gen. P.K. Chakravorty, VSM (retd)
and Brig. Gurmeet Kanwal (retd)

'The Battle of Haji Pir is a tale of determined leadership at a tactical level. As all battles in the mountains go, this one was fought against two adversaries—the Pakistan Army and inclement weather and terrain. Meticulous coordination between units and formations won us this famous victory. It is tragic that we ceded the captured bulge at Tashkent.'

—Maj. Gen. Neeraj Bali, SM (retd)

'The Battle of Haji Pir during the 1965 Indo–Pak war stands as a testament to India's audacity, with the elite 1 Para leading a series of courageous attacks unparalleled in military history. Multiple battalions showcased valour, resulting in numerous sacrifices by dedicated officers, JCOs and gallant men. Their collective acts of courage led to the capture of the Haji Pir Pass, immortalizing this battle as one of India's most heroic post-1947.'

—Maj. Gen. Paramjit Singh Sandhu,
AVSM, VSM (veteran)

'*The capture of the Haji Pir Pass and establishing the Uri–Poonch link-up during the 1965 war were an astounding success. It remains a classic offensive undertaken by an infantry brigade in the mountains.*'

—**Brig. Shamsher Singh, AVSM (retd)**

To my father, Rao Digh Ram Yadav, who passed away on 31 March 2021. His memory is a constant source of love and inspiration, guiding me each day

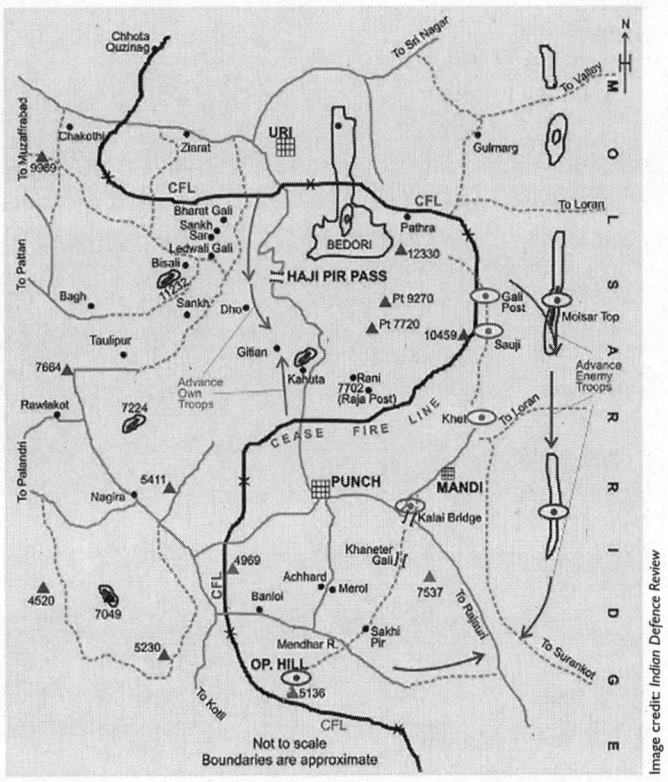

Image credit: Indian Defence Review

If you look at the map carefully, you will realize that the land mass between the towns of Uri and Poonch is with Pakistan. This land mass is called the 'Haji Pir bulge' and in August 1965, the Indian Army not only captured the Haji Pir Pass, but also connected the towns of Uri and Poonch, thereby capturing the entire bulge area of 500 sq. km.

PREFACE

On 5 August 1965, more than 30,000 Pakistani infiltrators crossed the Cease-Fire Line (CFL) which divided POK (Pakistan-occupied Kashmir) and Jammu and Kashmir, and began attacking the local people and Army and government infrastructure. The infiltrators comprised trained militia, mercenaries, Razakars (paramilitary force of volunteers) and regular Pakistan Army personnel.

The operation was code-named 'Gibraltar' and was conceived by Major General (Maj. Gen.) Akhtar Hussain Malik, the commander of 12 Division of the Pakistan Army, and Zulfikar Ali Bhutto, then foreign minister of Pakistan; it was approved by Field Marshal Mohammed Ayub Khan, the President of Pakistan.

The infiltrators, divided into six forces, intended to attack Kashmir from six different sectors, and the code names of these forces were Tariq, Qasim, Khalid, Salahuddin, Ghaznavi and Babur. These forces were headed by a brigadier-rank officer of the Pakistan Army. The mission of these infiltrators was to mingle with the local people and destroy roads, hospitals, cantonments, schools, bridges—basically any structure that was a symbol of India-led modernization. Pakistani planners were of the opinion that the Kashmiri people would welcome the infiltrators and join them in creating a tsunami of unrest, which the Indian government would not be able to contain.

By the end of August, the infiltrators and the local people would converge on Srinagar and capture the airport and radio station. After this, the infiltrators would announce that Kashmir was no longer a part of India and declare a 'revolutionary council' as the caretaker custodians of the Kashmir state.

This revolutionary council would then seek international support for Kashmir to be recognized as an independent country and Pakistan would be the first country to announce its support. Even the speech that would be read out by this puppet council was given to the Pakistani infiltrators (placed in the photo section).

The plan was so secret that Indian intelligence had no clue of it. Consequently, as the killings, lootings and destruction of infrastructure began on 5 August 1965 in Kashmir, the Indian government, which was still nursing the wounds of its humiliating defeat to China in 1962, was totally blindsided. Before the Indians could lift their heads and organize resources, considerable damage had been caused and the Pakistanis' devilish plan seemed to be working.

Meanwhile, the government of Pakistan went all out to plant misleading stories in global news networks saying what was happening in Kashmir was a local uprising of the Kashmiri people, who were fed up with Indian rule.

But the Pakistani commanders had made two errors in their calculations—one, they had misjudged the loyalty of the Kashmiri people and two, they had underestimated the courage and professionalism of the Indian Army.

When the Indian Army was losing ground initially, the Western Army Commander, Lieutenant General (Lt Gen.) Harbaksh Singh, proposed crossing the CFL and capturing the Haji Pir bulge, an area of approximately 500 sq. km. His decision to go on the offensive instead of remaining defensive was approved by General (Gen.) J.N. Chaudhuri, the coursemate of Field Marshal Ayub Khan. This manoeuvre not only successfully blocked the infiltration through the Haji Pir Pass, but also locked the infiltrators within India, making them either panic and surrender or face the Indian Army, which could hunt them down and liquidate them.

The name of the officer who led the troops of 1 Para Battalion to capture the formidable Haji Pir Pass was Major (Maj.) Ranjit Singh Dyal. The companies he led were of a mixed martial composition: Alpha Company, comprising jawans belonging to the Sikh community, Bravo Company, comprising jawans belonging to the Dogra community, Charlie Company, comprising jawans belonging to the Jat community, and Delta Company, comprising jawans belonging to the Ahir community.

At the operational and tactical levels, the operation was conducted by Brigadier (Brig.) Zorawar Chand Bakshi, the brigade commander, and Lieutenant Colonel (Lt Col) Prabjinder Singh, the battalion commander, besides the other officers, JCOs and jawans of 1 Para Battalion. The attack from the Uri side was called 'Operation Bakshi'. In addition to 1 Para, other battalions that participated in this battle, which turned the tables on Pakistan, were 19 Punjab, 4 Rajput, 6 Dogra (joined later), 4 Sikh Light Infantry and 6 JAK Rifles.

While the primary focus of the book is the northern assault from Uri, leading to the capture of the Haji Pir Pass in POK, I have also included the attack from the south, code-named 'Operation Faulad', from the Poonch side. It was only through the successful link-up from the south that India managed to secure the entire landmass referred to as the Haji Pir bulge.

The Battle of Haji Pir narrates the extraordinary tale of these courageous officers and jawans, a narrative with few parallels in the history of the Indian armed forces. There was a total of fifteen battalion attacks by the Indian Army in the entire Haji Pir campaign, which lasted twenty-eight days.

However, a surprising turn of events unfolded that caught not only the Indian Army but the entire nation off guard. Despite the victorious end to the Battle of Haji Pir, where India took control of the entire 500-sq.-km Haji Pir bulge, a twist occurred due to a strategic move by the Indian government. On 10 January 1966, amid a UN-brokered peace agreement in Tashkent, India handed back control of the entire Haji Pir bulge to Pakistan. This decision was based on Pakistan's assurances that the pass would not be used for infiltration. Ironically, the Haji Pir Pass remains a preferred route for terrorists and troublemakers, undermining the peace process in the Kashmir Valley to this day.

Therefore, despite India's victory in the battle and the subsequent return of the captured territory, the unresolved challenges associated with the Haji Pir Pass continue to pose a threat to the stability and tranquillity of the region to this day. The misuse of this strategic route by elements seeking to undermine peace highlights the complexities and ongoing struggles in the delicate geopolitical landscape of the Kashmir Valley.

Before concluding, I want to explain why I decided to write this book. After publishing my book *The Battle of Rezang La* in 2021, my curiosity led me to study the events of the 1965 war with Pakistan. Childhood memories from visits to my maternal village, Bewal, in Haryana's Mahendragarh district, were filled with stories of Lance Havildar (L/Hav.) Umrao Singh's bravery. Umrao Singh, a posthumous recipient of the Vir Chakra award, belonged to the Delta Company of 1 Para Battalion and played a crucial role in capturing the Haji Pir Pass. He hailed from Surjanwas, a village adjacent to Bewal.

What began as modest research evolved into an effort that lasted more than two years. Immersed in the subject, I visited the 1 Para Battalion in Nahan, Himachal Pradesh, where I meticulously analysed archived records, pictures, books and journals. Later, I read news articles, anecdotes and blogs by defence experts and watched various videos, besides interviewing officers, JCOs and jawans who had knowledge of this battle. My quest extended to engaging with survivors and family members, enriching my understanding of the historical narrative. The acknowledgements section highlights the individuals I had the privilege of meeting during this endeavour.

It's worth noting that the accounts of this battle found in various sources exhibit slight variations. To ensure a comprehensive representation, I have drawn primarily upon four key sources: 'Official War History, 1965', History Division, Ministry of Defence, Government of India; *War Despatches: Indo–Pak Conflict, 1965* by Lt Gen. Harbaksh Singh, the Western Army Commander overseeing this operation and the originator of this battle; *The Monsoon War: Young Officers Reminisce—1965 India–Pakistan War* by Captain (Capt.) Amarinder Singh and Lt Gen. Tajindar Shergill; and personal experiences narrated by Brig. Arvinder Singh, who fought in this battle as the company commander of Delta Company in the rank of major and was injured in the process. Additionally, I read numerous books and research pieces on the subject, cross-referencing them with survivor accounts wherever possible. A detailed bibliography is appended at the conclusion of the book.

Jai Hind!

Kulpreet Yadav
Commandant (retd)
10 February 2024

PART 1

To annex Kashmir, Pakistan launches top-secret operation code-named 'Gibraltar'

1

MUREE, PAKISTAN, 15 MAY 1965

A convoy of military vehicles snaked its way on the winding roads of Murree, the picturesque hill station in the heart of Punjab, Pakistan. Leading the procession was a staff car displaying five stars on both front and rear, surrounded by motorcycle-riding uniformed soldiers. Following closely were four more staff cars, with motorcyclists in uniform ensuring the security of the rear of the convoy. The scene conveyed a sense of strength and precision.

As the VVIP convoy meandered towards its destination, Field Marshal Mohammed Ayub Khan, the President of Pakistan, observed the landscape from within the car with five stars. Murree provided a welcome respite from the heat of the plains, and at an elevation of 7000 feet, the temperature stood at a refreshing 12 degrees Celsius.

The convoy passed through the entrance of the 12 Infantry Division headquarters, an imposing compound

3

encircled by towering walls. Sentries armed with automatic rifles gazed down from watchtowers located above the fortress-like barricades.

The car with the five stars came to a halt under the porch and an army jawan saluted smartly before bending to open the door. The Field Marshal climbed out. A huge man who weighed around 100 kg and stood over 6 feet 3 inches tall, getting out seemed to be an effort for him.

As he looked up, the officers who stood in a line waiting for him jointly saluted and said, 'Good morning, Mr President.'

'Good morning.'

He first shook the hand of Maj. Gen. Akhtar Hussain Malik, the General Officer Commanding (GOC) of 12 Infantry Division. After this, Maj. Gen. Malik introduced him to the other five officers of 12 Division who stood on his left and the Field Marshal shook hands with them too.

Meanwhile, from the other staff cars that had stopped behind the President's car, emerged three flag-rank officers. These were Maj. Gen. Malik Sher Bahadur, the Chief of General Staff (CGS); Brig. Gul Hassan, the Director of Military Operations (DMO); and Brig. Sayyed Ahmed Irshad, the Director of Military Intelligence (DMI).

From the car that had no stars climbed out a sprightly man in a suit and a tie. This was Zulfikar Ali Bhutto, Pakistan's foreign minister, a young and powerful, foreign-educated minister who was only thirty-seven years old at the time.

'This way, sir.' Maj. Gen. Malik led the entourage after he had shaken hands with the other flag officers and Mr Bhutto.

They walked on a red carpet through a brightly lit corridor that was lined on both sides with brass pots holding flowers until they reached the door marked 'Conference Room'.

Maj. Gen. Malik stepped aside and said, 'After you, sir.'

The Field Marshal entered the conference room, walked to the head of the table and sat down in the chair earmarked for him. Within seconds, everyone else sat down in the chairs designated for them too.

'Permission to begin, sir?' Maj. Gen. Malik asked the Field Marshal.

'Yes.'

'Sir, welcome to the Headquarters 12 Infantry Division—'

'Let's cut to the chase, General. Speed, I want speed. Action!' the Field Marshal cut in.

'Right, sir. The agenda for today is to present a foolproof plan to make Kashmir a part of Pakistan.'

Field Marshal Ayub Khan looked up sharply and smiled. He turned to look at Bhutto, who nodded. Then he looked at Maj. Gen. Malik Sher Bahadur, who stared back at him stone-faced.

The Field Marshal brought his attention back to Maj. Gen. Malik and said, 'That's the dream of every Pakistani, isn't it? Fire away, General!'

Maj. Gen. Malik's back straightened and his chest inflated as he continued, 'Sir, we have prepared a fail-safe operation—'

'What's the code name of this operation?'

'It's called Operation Gibraltar, sir.'

'Operation Gibraltar?'

Bhutto cleared his throat and Field Marshal Ayub Khan turned to look at him.

Bhutto began, 'Sir, may I?'

Ayub Khan nodded.

'Sir, as the President knows, the Muslim conquest of the Iberian Peninsula, that is, present-day Spain and Portugal, was launched from Gibraltar in the ninth century.'

'I know, I know . . . but how is it related here?'

'My President, our Gibraltar operation will free the Kashmiris from the Hindus forever. It will establish the rule of Muslims over Kashmir, the way Muslims established their rule in Spain and Portugal.'

The President turned to look at Maj. Gen. Malik Sher Bahadur and asked, 'General, what do you think?'

'Sir, I had received this plan a few weeks ago and after careful analysis at the Army headquarters, I have come to the conclusion that this is not a viable plan in the present circumstances.'

Bhutto started to speak, 'General Sher Bahadur, sir, with due respect, I don't think you see the larger picture here. In 1962, India was crushed by China. We should have attacked them soon after the war. But we missed that opportunity. Now, India is expanding its forces like never before. In another two years, their army will be one million-plus. The Americans have given a lot of aid to the Indians, over 100 million dollars, and the Russians are helping them too. The Indians are consolidating as we speak. If we have to hit them, we have to hit them now and hit them hard.'

Maj. Gen. Malik added, 'Sir, I want to draw your attention to the Kutch skirmish that took place a few months ago. India's response to our aggression was lukewarm. It's clear—after 1962, India is scared of war.'

The Field Marshal asked, 'What exactly is your plan, General Malik?'

'Sir, I agree with Major General Sher Bahadur, and therefore, we don't want a full-scale war. Our plan involves the militia, volunteers from Azad Kashmir and the local people in Indian-held Kashmir who are ready to fight the Indian Army and the government's machinery.'

The Field Marshal smiled, 'A half war . . . something like what we did in Kutch? Is that what your plan is, General?'

Bhutto replied before Maj. Gen. Malik could. 'Exactly, sir. When India starts crying, we will tell the world that it is not us. That it is a local uprising of the Kashmiris. While we exploit India's timidity, we will use propaganda and mind games to wrest Kashmir away from them once and for all.'

Field Marshal Ayub Khan considered this for a few seconds and said, 'What if it becomes a full-blown war?'

Bhutto said, 'Sir, we are in a strong position for that, too. Because we are now members of SEATO and CENTO, the western powers will have no option but to help us militarily.'

Maj. Gen. Malik added, 'And sir, let's not forget, China has promised to attack India's borders to divert their attention if a full-scale war does break out with us. And India can never fight a war on two fronts simultaneously.'

'Hmm . . . so we have nothing to worry about? How far have we reached with our training of the guerrillas?'

'Sir, we have been training them for months now and I think they are ready to sacrifice their lives for our land and for Islam. We are ready in every respect, sir, and the detailed plan is complete for your review in the SMR (Sand Model Room).'

'Let's go!' The President rose to his feet.

Maj. Gen. Malik led the President to the next room, which was marked 'Sand Model Room'. They entered the large rectangular hall. Chairs had been arranged against the

walls all around the room and in the middle of the hall was a
2 feet-deep rectangular pit.

A three-dimensional terrain of the entire Kashmir region
had been prepared with sand in this pit, complete with snow-
capped peaks, mountain passes, valleys, prominent watershed
features like rivers and hill contours, towns, cantonments,
airfields, dams, bridges, roads, jungles and the force
disposition of both the Indian Army and the Pakistan Army.

To facilitate the map-to-ground and ground-to-map
correlation by commanders during mission planning, detailed
one-inch and quarter-inch maps had been displayed on the
wall with powerful lights focused on them.

The Field Marshal stood at the edge of the pit with the
others on both sides.

His eyes focused on the sand model of Kashmir, Field
Marshal Ayub Khan, the President of Pakistan, said, 'Okay,
brief me about Operation Gibraltar.'

With the help of a wooden pointer, Maj. Gen. Malik
shared his plan in detail over the next one hour. No one
interrupted him.

When he finished, the Field Marshal said, 'Before I speak
my mind, I want to know the reaction of the others. Let's
begin with the officers from 12 Division. Colonel (GS) and
Colonel (Q), what do you think? . . . Don't look at your boss,
tell me the truth. I want honest answers.'

The staff officers, realizing that the entire top brass of
the Pakistan Army was staring at them, didn't flinch. One
by one, both said that it was a great plan with zero chance
of failure.

'Hmm,' said the President, 'and Major General Sher
Bahadur, what do you think of it now?'

'Sir, it's a good plan . . . and I don't doubt the commitment and professionalism of General Malik and his 12 Infantry Division. Theoretically speaking, this is a good plan, but I think we are banking a lot on the Chinese, the Americans, the Russians and indeed the members of SEATO and CENTO to come to our rescue, but what if they don't? Let's face it, Mr President, India's and Pakistan's militaries are unequal. We do have better aircraft and tanks now, we know, but India has acquired a lot after 1962, so it's not entirely in our favour.'

Field Marshal Ayub Khan laughed heartily. After a few seconds, everyone else joined him.

He stopped as suddenly as he had started and the others stopped too.

Then Field Marshal Ayub Khan spoke, his voice charged and louder than before, 'I want everyone to know that whatever Major General Sher Bahadur has said is all true. I'm not doubting his patriotism even one bit. But, when it comes to war, the most important things are not tanks and aircraft. The most important thing is *courage*. We Pakistanis are a martial race, while Hindus are timid. It is the Muslim kings who have ruled the Hindus, and not vice versa. The question really is this: Is Pakistan afraid of the five-foot two-inch Shastri and his Hindu military?'

Everyone stared back at him, not knowing how to react. This was the first time the President had shown his true character by expressing himself in an authoritative voice. His face was now shining due to the effort and his eyes were sparkling.

Field Marshal Ayub Khan, the President of Pakistan, asked again, 'Tell me, are you afraid of the Indians?'

'No, sir!' everyone shouted back this time.

The Field Marshal took a deep breath and said, his voice better controlled now, 'Let's free Kashmir, General Malik. I approve Operation Gibraltar. No more dithering now. I want everyone to fall in line.'

With that, he walked out of the SMR, Maj. Gen. Malik right behind him. The others left the room too.

The entourage walked to the officers' mess, located next to the Division headquarters' building, where a lavish lunch awaited them. Everyone ate gladly. The smiles on Maj. Gen. Malik's and Bhutto's faces, seated next to one another, were the widest. History was about to be made. Pakistan was now just a few months away from capturing Kashmir.

The D-Day approved by the president for Operation Gibraltar was 5 August 1965 and the committee to execute it comprised the GOC, 12 Infantry Division, CGS, DMO and DMI.

(After the 1965 Indo–Pak war) General Mohammad Musa, the Chief of Army Staff (COAS), Pakistan, was asked by a senior Indian correspondent, Kuldip Nayar, why Operation Gibraltar was conceived and launched, leading to the various stages of escalation. He has been reported to have said, 'Ask the President.' When Field Marshal Ayub Khan, the President of Pakistan, was asked the same question, he answered, 'Ask Bhutto.' When Bhutto was asked, to his credit he readily agreed that he was for it.

Ayub had been convinced by Bhutto that in a war with India, the Chinese would come to Pakistan's aid. Cheng Yi, the Chinese foreign minister, had on various occasions hinted at such support, but without any specific commitment. Finally, it was the belief that Indians would not cross the international border, and that the average Kashmiri would welcome the infiltrators with open arms, which led to the decision being taken. Another strange belief has always been that the Muslim soldier was far superior to what they term 'the Hindu army'. These collective assumptions finally led to Pakistan taking the offensive.

—*Capt. Amarinder Singh and Lt Gen. Tajindar Shergill,*
The Monsoon War: Young Officers Reminisce—
1965 India–Pakistan War

2

SRINAGAR, JAMMU AND KASHMIR, INDIA, 1 AUGUST 1965

Lt Gen. Harbaksh Singh, the general officer commanding in chief (GOC-in-C) of the Indian Army's Western Command, and Corps Commander Lt Gen. Kashmir Singh Katoch stood together on the Srinagar airport tarmac. It was the first day of August, and at ten in the morning, the temperature was a pleasant 19 degrees Celsius.

Awaiting the just-landed AN-12 aircraft of the Indian Air Force, the two flag-rank officers were joined by dignitaries from various state departments of Jammu and Kashmir, each holding flowers.

Lt Gen. Harbaksh Singh, having assumed the duties of GOC-in-C in November 1963, was a tall, decorated officer with a remarkable history. He had spent three and a half years as a prisoner of war in Japanese custody during World War II and had played a significant role in the first Kashmir war in 1947–48, earning a Vir Chakra for his bravery in capturing Tithwal.

Without turning to Lt Gen. Katoch, Lt Gen. Harbaksh Singh remarked, keeping his eyes on the taxiing aircraft, 'The day is finally here, General Katoch! Although it took the Army headquarters over a year to decide on my proposal.'

'That's correct, sir. In the end, I believe your experience in the Valley during 1947–48 nailed it.'

Lt Gen. Harbaksh Singh turned to his Corps Commander, saying, 'General Katoch, even though it's been almost two decades since I last fought in the Kashmir Valley, as a young officer, I spent a lot of time gaining first-hand knowledge of the terrain, especially the mountain routes likely to be used by the enemy.'

'Exactly, sir. Not much has changed in these years.'

Lt Gen. Harbaksh Singh, focused on the aircraft again, replied, 'A few things might have changed on our side of Kashmir, General, but nothing has certainly changed in the attitude of the Pakistanis.'

'Yes, sir.'

A dignitary caught Lt Gen. Harbaksh Singh's eye. Waving back, he continued, 'That's why, after taking over the command, I realized that this "penny-packet" manning of posts along the 640 kilometres of the CFL border is not only inadequate but also tactically weak.'

Lt Gen. Katoch inhaled deeply and responded, 'And this was the precise reason why we lost to China three years ago. Therefore, sir, your proposal is spot on. The enemy would certainly use the Haji Pir Pass in the Uri–Poonch bulge to enter the Kashmir Valley.'

The two generals fell silent after this. Another recommendation by Lt Gen. Harbaksh Singh was to replace the undertrained personnel manning border posts, currently staffed by police and home guard battalions, with the J&K militia. This needed urgent recruitment.

After internal discussions and meetings in Delhi, Army Chief Gen. J.N. Chaudhuri decided to visit Srinagar on 1 August 1965, with a single agenda—a decisive meeting to strengthen the security of Jammu and Kashmir based on Lt Gen. Harbaksh Singh's recommendations.

As soon as the AN-12 stopped, the door opened and Gen. J.N. Chaudhuri stepped out.

Lt Gen. Harbaksh Singh and Lt Gen. Katoch saluted the tall Chief of Army Staff. He smartly returned their salute. Then, as he neared them, he shook their hands and, after accepting the flowers, the hands of others present too.

Within minutes, the three generals were being driven to a high-security Army unit in Srinagar for a meeting behind closed doors.

Once they had settled down in a secure room that had been prepared for this meeting, Gen. J.N. Chaudhuri said, 'General Harbaksh, we had a lot of discussions in Delhi about your proposal and the changes you want to better the security of Kashmir.'

'That's good news. What's the decision, sir?'

'Well, we agree with your suggestions that we need better trained local Kashmiris in the Army as they are better suited for the security of our border. But, as you know, recruitment is a time-consuming process. Until then, what do you suggest?'

Lt Gen. Harbaksh Singh replied, 'Sir, I agree, recruitment will take time, but we should start the process without any further delay. And until then, we should keep training hard and be prepared for the worst.'

Gen. J.N. Chaudhuri nodded and turned to look at Lt Gen. Katoch.

Lt Gen. Katoch added, 'Sir, I think we need to augment our force in Kashmir quickly, because here we have enemies on both sides—Pakistan in the west and China in the east and the north.'

'I agree. Since 1962, India has been doing all that it can. Emergency recruitment is going on round the clock, training periods at all levels have been truncated, new academies have been commissioned and more. I see your point of augmenting the XV Corps in Kashmir, but we need to look at all our borders. For example, who knew Pakistan would send a full division into Kutch like they did earlier this year while we had just half a brigade there?'

After a few more points, the meeting was over. Lt Gen. Harbaksh Singh and Lt Gen. Katoch were glad that Gen. Chaudhuri was on the same page as them on the planning and the conduct of action and counter-action. A united top leadership like this was ideal for any army in the world. But, as yet unknown to them, the two commanders were just days away from disagreeing in their approach to defending Kashmir.

The next morning, the Chief of Army Staff, the Army Commander and the Corps Commander met the civil dignitaries of Jammu and Kashmir state in a planned 'military-civil' conference in Srinagar. The conference room had more than a dozen people.

After a full day of deliberations, it was decided that four additional battalions of J&K militia would be raised immediately, and once ready, these battalions would take over the border posts from the police, home guards and the Army.

Evidently, the Chief of Army Staff had endorsed the Army Commander's plan and put his seal of approval on it. But, as the coming weeks would prove, this decision would turn out to be too little, too late. At that time, though, barely days away from a major strike by Pakistan, which would nearly take the Kashmir Valley away from India forever, the generals and the civil administration had no clue what the future held for them.

To Pakistan's credit, Operation Gibraltar was not only meticulously planned and devious, it was such a well-guarded secret that not even their own Army, outside of 12 Division, had any clue about it.

3

HEADQUARTERS, 1 PARA BATTALION, URI, KASHMIR, 2 AUGUST 1965

Lt Col G.A. Wright, the commanding officer (CO) of 1 Para Battalion, emerged from his office, flanked by two jawans escorting him. An officer of British origin, he had been awarded the Vir Chakra for his bravery during the 1947 operations in Jammu and Kashmir.

It was a poignant day for Lt Col G.A. Wright. He had opted to remain in India even after its independence, patiently awaiting his command of 1 Para, rather than return to Britain. Now, on the eve of relinquishing command to his successor, Lt Col G.A. Wright stood at the threshold of bidding farewell to his beloved 1 Para Battalion and, indeed, to India itself, as he prepared to relocate to Britain for resettlement.

He arrived at the cantonment grounds where his battalion had gathered for a special Sainik Sammelan and barakhana. Approximately 700 jawans sat in meticulous rows on sheets spread out on the ground, while the Junior Commissioned Officers (JCOs) and officers occupied camp stools on their respective sides.

At the forefront of the assembled soldiers were arranged a table and two chairs, with the senior-most JCO of the battalion, the subedar major (SM), standing beside one chair and the battalion adjutant standing beside the other.

Spotting the CO, Maj. Ranjit Singh Dyal, the Second-in-Command (2 i/c) of the battalion, stepped forward and delivered a crisp salute. The CO returned the salute and awaited the report.

'Battalion *aapke special* Sainik Sammelan *ke liye taiyyar hai, srimaan.* Seven hundred jawans, twenty-five JCOs and ten officers are present.'

Lt Col Wright took his seat, with the battalion adjutant and the SM beside him. A hush fell over the gathering; all eyes were fixed on the CO.

The CO of 1 Para started to speak, his voice loud and clear: '1 Para *ke bahadur* officers, JCO *saheban aur mere pyaare jawano, aaj mera aap sab ke saath yeh aakhri din hai. Har* officer *ka sapna hota hai ki woh jis paltan mein bharti hua hai, usko wahi paltan ki* command *karne ka mauka mile. Main un* lucky officers *mein se ek hoon* (Brave officers of 1 Para, respected JCOS and my dear soldiers, today is my last day with you. It is every officer's dream that he should get the opportunity to command the unit he has been commissioned into. I'm one such fortunate officer).'

He paused, his eyes scanning the familiar faces, who looked at him impassively, before continuing, '*Humne teen saal saath-saath kaam kiya hai. Aapki mehnat aur himmat ki wajah se saare* operations *ko bakhoobi anjaam diya hai.*

1 Para Indian Army *ki sabse bahadur paltan hai* (We have worked together for three years. Because of your hard work and courage, we have accomplished all operations very well. 1 Para is the bravest battalion of the Indian Army).'

The jawans started to clap. The CO stopped speaking, letting the tide of emotion subside.

Lt Col Wright continued, '1 Para *ki sabse khoobsurat baat yeh hai ki hamare paas Hindustan ki chaar sabse bahadur kaumein hain.* Alpha Company *mein sherdil* Sikh *hain* (The best part of 1 Para is that we have the four bravest communities of India. In Alpha Company we have the lion-hearted Sikhs).'

The jawans of Alpha Company, who were Sikh soldiers, shouted, '*Bharat Mata ki jai* (Long live mother India)!'

'Bravo Company *mein janbaaz* Dogra *hain* (In Bravo Company, we have the daring Dogras).'

The jawans of Bravo Company, who belonged to the Dogra community, shouted, '*Bharat Mata ki jai!*'

'Charlie Company *mein joshiley* Jat *hain* (In Charlie Company, we have the courageous Jats).'

The jawans of Charlie Company, who belonged to the Jat community, shouted, '*Bharat Mata ki jai!*'

'*Aur* Delta Company *mein veer* Ahir *hain* (in Delta Company we have the brave Ahirs).'

The jawans of Delta Company, who belonged to the Ahir community, shouted, '*Bharat Mata ki jai!*'

After sharing a few heartfelt experiences, the CO stopped speaking and stood up, prompting everyone present to follow suit. Accompanied by the battalion adjutant and SM, the CO strolled along the rows of jawans, engaging in informal conversations.

Tables were arranged on the sides, one for the officers and several long ones for the jawans, each neatly adorned with paper plates. Consisting of two ball-shaped pakoras (called bonda) and two jalebis, the plates were uniform for everyone. At the SM's signal, all the jawans picked up their plates while the company commanders and battalion officers collected theirs from the officers' table.

Alpha Company was led by Maj. Harsh Yadav, Bravo by Maj. H. Patil, Charlie by Maj. J.C.M. Rao and Delta by Maj. Arvinder Singh Baicher. Besides Maj. Ranjit Singh Dyal, the 2 i/c, additional officers present included Maj. Vaswani, Capt. M.M.P.S. Dhillon, Capt. J.S. Bindra, the adjutant, Capt. Gurung, the quartermaster and Lt Ranganathan. As the company commanders rejoined their respective units, the other officers mingled with the jawans.

Lt Col Wright went from company to company, conversing with the jawans, employing humour to lighten the mood and offering words of praise for their collective achievements. As he moved, he casually sampled a pakora from one jawan's plate and a jalebi from another, showcasing the close bond between the CO and his troops, a hallmark of Indian Army battalions' vibrant cohesiveness and team spirit.

However, within some sections of the battalion, murmurs could be heard. While the CO was undeniably popular, there was another officer who commanded immense admiration—the 2 i/c, Maj. Ranjit Singh Dyal. Born on 15 November 1928, in the village of Teokar in Kurukshetra district, Punjab (now in Haryana), Maj. Dyal, despite being in his late thirties, remained unmarried and wholly devoted to his battalion. Officers sometimes joked that he was married to the Army. Maj. Dyal joined the 50 Para Brigade as a brigade major after completing staff college. After two years, he was appointed as the 2 i/c in 1 Para in January 1965.

Thus, when the jawans learnt of the appointment of a new officer, Lt Col Prabjinder Singh, as the commanding officer of 1 Para, shock rippled through the ranks. The expectation had been for Maj. Dyal to be promoted and given command.

While the barakhana unfolded, Lt Col Prabjinder Singh, having arrived a day earlier, awaited the formal takeover of 1 Para's command the next day, on 3 August 1965, from Lt Col G.A. Wright. Lt Col Prabjinder Singh had arrived from New Delhi, where he was the military assistant to Paramasiva Prabhakar Kumaramangalam, the Vice Chief of the Army.

4

HEADQUARTERS, 161 MOUNTAIN BRIGADE, BARAMULLA, KASHMIR, 3 AUGUST 1965

Brig. M.K. Balachandran, the brigade commander of 161 Mountain Brigade, was engrossed in reading the newspaper when his PA informed him over the intercom, 'Sir, division commander is on the line.'

Setting aside the newspaper, Brig. Balachandran picked up the phone and said, 'Good morning, sir.'

'Good morning, Bala, how are you?' inquired Maj. Gen. Swarup Singh Kalaan, the GOC of 19 Division.

'Very well, sir. Thank you!'

'Is the change of command of 1 Para complete?'

'Yes, sir. The outgoing and incoming COs are on their way to my office right now for my approval and signatures.'

'Hmm . . . I'm surprised that the Army headquarters chose to ignore Major Dyal.'

'Yes, sir. It came as a surprise to me as well. I was confident that Major Dyal was ready.'

'Keep a close eye on the new CO. We are right on the border, and you know what Pakistan did in Kutch earlier this year.'

'Of course, sir. And I know Colonel Prabjinder well. I'm sure he will keep the battalion in top shape, just like his predecessor.'

'Great!' The GOC disconnected the call. Brig. M.K. Balachandran placed the phone down, lines of worry etched on his forehead.

At that moment there was a knock on his door and the brigade commander called out, 'Come in!'

The door opened and the brigade's adjutant ushered in Lt Col W.A. Wright, the outgoing CO of 1 Para, and Lt Col Prabjinder Singh, the new CO of 1 Para. They both smartly saluted the commander.

Brig. Balachandran, now on his feet, returned their salute and gestured to them to take their seats. 'Congratulations,' he said after all three had sat down.

'Thank you, sir,' the two officers replied in unison, both grateful for different reasons. One had successfully completed his command, while the other had assumed command of a prestigious battalion of the Indian Army, a coveted appointment.

'Lieutenant Colonel Singh, are you satisfied with the state of the men and weapons in 1 Para?'

'Yes, sir. The battalion is in great shape. I'm very fortunate to be commanding the battalion I was commissioned into.'

'Right, you indeed are. And Lieutenant Colonel Wright, how does this make you feel?'

'Emotional, sir. 1 Para boys are special. They are like family to me. It will take me months, if not years, to get over this.'

'So what's your plan after this?'

'I'm hoping to pack my bags and move to England soon.'

'Well, best wishes. Do you have the handing-taking over notes ready?'

'Yes, sir.'

Lt Col Wright opened the register he was carrying and placed it in front of the brigade commander. The two officers had already signed the open page. All that remained was for Brig. Balachandran to sign and formally approve the change of command of 1 Para Battalion.

After a brief discussion, the brigade commander signed the register and handed it back, then called for tea. Over tea, Brig. Balachandran remarked, 'Colonel Prabjinder, at the moment, our area is calm. There's no intelligence about Pakistan trying to stir up any mischief.'

'Right, sir.'

'But, as you know, these Pakistanis are a tricky lot. What they did in Kutch was completely unexpected. It's August now, but Pakistan has already violated the CFL 1800 times, that is 522 times more than in 1964. So we won't know anything until we are right in it.'

'Sir, my focus will be on being battle-ready at all times. All the nine picquets on the border manned by 1 Para will be on their toes round the clock.'

'That's the spirit. As you know, the more we sweat in peace, the less we bleed in war.'

After a few more minutes, the two officers saluted the brigade commander and departed.

In the early 1950s, as part of its strategy to counter the influence of the Soviet Union and its Communist ideology, the United States established various military alliances, including the North Atlantic Treaty Organization (NATO), Central Treaty Organization (CENTO) and Southeast Asia Treaty Organization (SEATO). The primary objective was for member nations to collaborate and pool resources to safeguard themselves against the expansionist aims of the Soviet Union.

Enticed by promises of military and economic support, smaller nations willingly joined these alliances. Pakistan, a newly formed nation emerging from British India, seized this opportunity and became a member of CENTO and SEATO in 1955. In contrast, India pursued a non-aligned stance. Pakistan reaped substantial benefits from its alliance memberships, receiving military aid totalling US$1.5 billion by 1965. This aid encompassed a wide array of modern military equipment, including Patton tanks, Sabre jets, F-104 Starfighter aircraft, MI rifles, Universal machine guns, mortars, recoilless rifles and various other defence apparatus.

Beyond equipment supply, Pakistani military officers underwent training in the United States. With a modernized military, collaboration with China, training of Azad Kashmir forces and the ascension to power through a coup of a Pakistan Army officer, Field Marshal and President Mohammed Ayub Khan, Pakistan sought to assert its strength and pursue territorial ambitions, particularly in the context of the Kashmir region.

PART 2

30,000 Pakistani infiltrators cross
border and attack key installations
in Kashmir

5

TANGMARG, NEAR GULMARG, KASHMIR, 5 AUGUST 1965

A young boy of around fifteen sat under a tree just outside a village called Dara Kassi. He was lazily staring at his herd of fifty-odd goats which were grazing in the lush meadow. The boy was humming a Kashmiri folk song, absent-mindedly moving the stick he was holding through the air.

The monsoon had been good that year and low clouds drifted around him. When one such mass of cloud lifted, he saw two strangers approaching him. Clearly, these men were strangers—he knew everyone who lived in the village.

The men stopped next to him, smiled and said, '*Salaam alaikum.*'

He smiled too and replied, '*Wa-alaikum-salaam.*'

The men were young, around twenty, he guessed, but their accent was different. They wore green salwar kameez and both had their hands behind them as if they were hiding something they didn't want him to see.

One of them asked, 'What's your name?'

'Mohammed Din.'

The man who had asked the name removed his hands from behind him. He was holding a gun. The boy, who had seen such guns only with the army and the police, stiffened.

'So, Mohammed Din, your village is in India or in Pakistan?'

The boy paused, as if wondering what to answer.

The same man continued, 'It's in India. But not for long. We are from Pakistan. We have come to liberate you.'

The boy stared back at them before he stammered and asked, 'Liberate?'

'Yes. And once you are free, the Hindus can never touch you.'

The boy looked away, nodding, trying to see if any of his goats had wandered away from the group.

The other man, who had not spoken so far, stepped forward and slapped him. The boy fell down.

This man hissed, 'When elders talk, you have to listen. These Hindus have turned you Kashmiris into mannerless animals.'

The first guy extended his hand and helped the boy get to his feet. Then he asked, 'How many Hindus are there in your village?'

The boy was shivering with fear by now. He shook his head.

'No Hindus? Okay, we want you to go to the village and tell everyone that Pakistani soldiers are here to save Kashmir from the Hindus.' He turned and pointed to a wooded area and continued, 'We are there. A hundred soldiers of Islam.

When we come tomorrow to the village, we should be welcomed with a feast. Our job is to burn the post office, damage the road, and blow up the bridge that's on the other side of your village. Clear?'

'Yes, sir.'

'You don't have to worry, Mohammed Din; once you are a part of Pakistan, you will be very happy.'

The second man smiled for the first time and said, 'Here, take these 400 rupees. And don't worry if a few of your goats go missing today. We can't fight this war on an empty stomach for you, can we?'

The boy took the money and nodded in understanding as the two men walked back towards the wooded area swinging their guns.

Even after the strangers with the guns had gone out of sight, Mohammed Din couldn't move for a few minutes. Finally, as his breathing stabilized, he felt something on his chin and touched it with his fingers. When he brought his fingers close to his face, he found his fingertips red. His nose was bleeding.

The next second, he turned sharply and started to run towards his village. He was no longer worried about his goats. All he had on his mind was to warn his countrymen in the minimum possible time.

Half an hour later, panting and out of breath, he was standing in front of the gate of the local Army's brigade headquarters.

The armed sepoy addressed him from behind the gate, 'Hey, young boy, what do you want?'

'*Sahab*, sahab, I have secret information that I want to share.'

'What is it?'

'Sahab, the information is very secret. I want to share it with a big sahab.'

'Get lost, young boy.'

'Sahab, sahab . . .'

Mohammed Din saw the sepoy moving away from the gate. He inhaled deeply and spoke in a loud voice, 'Sahab, it is about the Pakistan Army.'

The sepoy stopped mid-step and turned. He approached the gate again, levelled his gun at the young boy and asked, 'What about the Pakistan Army?'

'Sahab, I want to talk to someone senior. It's very important, trust me, and very secret.'

'Wait there.'

Behind the gate, the sepoy entered the small guard room made of tin and dialled a number.

'Sir, there is a local boy at the main gate. He is saying he has some information about the Pakistan Army . . . Yes, sir.'

A minute later, a naik approached the sepoy and peered at the boy through the gate. He didn't speak a word and instead retreated back into the headquarters.

A few minutes later, a company havildar major (CHM) approached the gate. He looked at the boy and asked, 'What's your name?'

'Mohammed Din, sahab.'

'And where are you from?'

'From Dara Kassi village, sahab.'

'Okay, tell me, what do you have?'

'*Shukriya*, sahab. But I want to speak to someone senior.'

'I'm senior.'

'Sahab, I want to speak to *jeepwala* sahab. It's about Pakistan, sahab. There is big trouble coming soon. We don't have time, sahab.'

The CHM stared hard at him and said, 'If you are bluffing like other boys of your age, we will punish you.'

The boy gulped and looked straight into the eyes of the CHM. Finally, the CHM turned and disappeared inside.

The boy paced the area outside the gate. He knew if he didn't get an audience with the right officer, and those two menacing-looking Pakistanis found out he had talked about them to the Army, not only would he be killed, but his sister, his father and his mother would be butchered too. His father had told him what the village and the families had to go through eighteen years ago, in 1947–48, when the Pakistanis had attacked for the first time. The Pakistanis were here once again to go on a rampage, killing locals and attacking the government and the soldiers. The thought depressed him and he started to pace more furiously.

The CHM was back after five minutes, although to the boy it seemed like an hour.

The sepoy he had spoken to first opened the gates and Mohammed Din was allowed to walk inside. Right at the gate, he was bodily patted down by the sepoy. Were they thinking he was carrying a bomb or a gun under his clothes? He brushed the thought aside and, for the first time in his life, walked inside the Army compound following the CHM.

The walled area was huge. There were many jeeps and motorcycles, and a shining black car was parked in front of the main building. As he walked, a few soldiers passed him, staring suspiciously. He waved at them nervously.

Finally, they stopped at the side of one of the buildings. A few feet from them, a young man in uniform sat in a camp chair. Before him, there was an empty camp chair, exactly like the one he was sitting on. There was no one else in sight.

The man in the chair looked up at Mohammed Din as he approached. There were three stars on his shoulders. This was the kind of big man the young boy wanted to speak to.

The officer spoke, 'Hello Mohammed Din. My name is Captain Kumar. Sit down.'

The officer pointed to the camp chair opposite him. This was completely unexpected and the young boy looked at him uncertainly.

'Sahab, I have secret information.'

'I'm sure you do. But first sit in the chair.'

'Sahab, how can I sit with you?'

'Yes, you can. Now, let's not waste each other's time. *Sit*!'

The young boy didn't move.

'SIT!' The captain raised his voice a bit.

The young boy sat down and looked at the captain, worried and confused.

The officer smiled and said, 'Yes, Mohammed Din, now tell me freely what you want to say.'

The young boy inhaled and said, 'Sir, what will I get in return for this information?'

The officer's smile didn't diminish.

He turned to look at the CHM, who was still standing next to them, and said, 'Get our guest 10 kilos atta, 5 kilos rice and some tea pouches.'

Then he put his hand in his pocket and pulled out a 100-rupee note. The officer extended it towards the young boy and said, 'Take this money too. Now, tell me.'

Instead of taking the money being offered, the young boy took out the money he had received from the strangers from his pocket. There were four new 100-rupee notes. He said, 'Sahab, today two strangers came to me. They had guns. They said Pakistan Army was here to help the Kashmiri people. They gave me this money to give information and prepare food for them.'

'You can keep that money and here, take this too.' The captain paused as the young boy pocketed the money, and then continued, 'Tell me, what did they look like?'

'Sir, there were two, wearing green salwar kameez, and their accent was different even though they spoke to me in Hindi.'

'And what exactly did they say?'

Mohammed Din narrated the conversation.

After he was done, the Captain was on his feet. Nodding to the CHM and patting the boy affectionately on his shoulder, the captain hurriedly walked into the building that had the shiny black car parked in front of it.

Fifteen minutes later, a platoon of around thirty armed Army jawans, led by Capt. Kumar, left for the area the boy had told them about. They reached there in another fifteen minutes.

The Pakistanis were caught off guard. A fierce encounter took place, which resulted in the Pakistani infiltrators escaping, leaving behind some of their arms and ammunition. The Indian Army decided not to chase them, to avoid being led into an inescapable ambush.

After the partition of India and Pakistan in 1947, the newly independent nations had disputes over various border areas. While Kashmir was undoubtedly the most contentious one, another major area of dispute that led to a military stand-off was the Rann of Kutch. Due to the peculiar nature of the Rann, it resembled a lake during the monsoons, turned into a marshy stretch of wilderness during the winters and became a blistered cake of dried earth during the summers. Consequently, the area had always remained uninhabited, incapable of supporting life in any form.

From January 1965 onwards, Pakistani forces started to cross the boundary to patrol the area controlled by India. This led to heated exchange of words and occasional firing between the patrol parties of both sides. As the consequent formal complaints of each government to the other didn't lead to any resolution, the territory, which had remained with India without any dispute from 1947 to 1965, turned into a disputed one and from April 1965, armed exchange between Indian forces and Pakistani forces began. The confrontation, which began between the Special Reserve Police (SRP) of Gujarat and Western Indus rangers of Pakistan, soon expanded to include the armies of both nations.

Finally, in June 1965, Harold Wilson, the Prime Minister of England, succeeded in persuading Lal Bahadur Shastri and Field Marshal Ayub Khan to stop hostilities and let an international tribunal arbitrate a decision to settle the boundary dispute. While India sent fifteen delegates for this arbitration, Pakistan sent thirteen.

The arbitration took almost three years and finally the Arbitration Tribunal's 1968 award gave 10 per cent of the disputed territory to Pakistan and the rest to India. This decision, while accepted by both parties, left lingering resentment and geopolitical tensions.

6

GALUTHI, MENDHAR, KASHMIR, 5 AUGUST 1962

A few hours after the incident involving Mohammed Din, Wazir Mohammed, a twenty-one-year-old man from village Dabrot near Galuthi in the Poonch sector, was walking towards his pear orchard when he was confronted by a few people with guns.

One of them asked, 'What is your name?'

The man who had spoken looked like their leader. Wazir counted seven of them standing in his way.

Wazir replied, 'Wazir Mohammed.'

The stranger said, 'We are from Pakistan. We have come to liberate you from India.'

Wazir gulped; all he could do was nod. The other men had their guns trained on his chest, their fingers on the trigger.

One of them extended money towards him as the man continued, 'We don't want to hurt you. All we want is

38

information about the Army locations. And when we come to the village tonight, we want food for twenty people. Can you do that?'

Wazir nodded. The men with the guns left.

Wazir pocketed the 300 rupees they had given him, turned and walked with purpose towards the nearest Army headquarters. An hour later, he was standing in front of the main gate of the 120 Brigade headquarters.

Inside, Brig. Bharat Singh, the brigade commander, had just learnt of the infiltration attempt that the Army had successfully countered near Tangmarg minutes earlier. The Corps Commander of the Jammu and Kashmir area, Lt Gen. Kashmir Singh Katoch, had sent a signal to all his divisions, and they had warned all their brigades in Kashmir to be extra vigilant. Something was certainly afoot.

That's when the battalion commander of 2 Garhwal Rifles rushed into Brig. Bharat Singh's office. After a smart salute, he said, 'Sir, there is a villager from Galuthi at the gate. He says he was approached by a few Pakistani men with guns.'

The brigadier looked up sharply and asked, 'That's not far from our headquarters, colonel. How many men did he say?'

'Sir, seven had met him, but they said there are more in the jungle and that they will come in the night to collect food from the village.'

'Food? How much food?'

'They said for twenty people.'

'Okay, send one of the company commanders with a platoon right away. We need to attack them before they expect us to. Who attacks first is important, colonel. *Now*!'

'Yes, sir. The Garhwalis are ready.'

The battalion commander saluted again and left the office.

Fifteen minutes later, Capt. Chander Narain Singh left the headquarters along with thirty-five men of his platoon. Soon, they reached the area that Wazir Mohammed had told them about. The sun had set, but there was sufficient light to make out the land features. Before the Indian platoon could even form up, the enemy greeted them with automatic fire from light machine guns (LMG) and medium machine guns (MMG).

The platoon commander was surprised by this. He was expecting only small arms fire. Clearly, these were no ordinary infiltrators—they were trained enemy soldiers. He ordered his men to take positions and fire back.

After the enemy was pinned down for a few minutes, Capt. C.N. Singh observed the area in detail. The enemy was strategically positioned at a higher level, as if they were expecting this attack. Perhaps they fed the information to Wazir for exactly this reaction from the Indian Army.

Thinking quickly, he decided to approach from the flanks as his soldiers continued to engage the enemy from the front. Capt. C.N. Singh knew that the only way to overcome the enemy was by silencing their LMG posts.

Crawling on his stomach as his troops kept firing, he stealthily approached the enemy from the side. After fifteen minutes, he could see one of the LMG posts of the enemy just 30 feet from him. He took aim with his gun and killed the Pakistani soldier manning it in one clean shot. The LMG fell silent and the captain retreated into the darkness. But there were more LMGs and a few MMGs in the deep too. The enemy was certainly more than twenty. In fact, he guessed over a hundred men.

After Capt. C.N. Singh had crawled back to his platoon, he ordered his jawans to stop firing. He made a new plan this time and divided the platoon into two parts. One, he ordered, would be led by him, and the other by a JCO.

As part of his strategy, the attack was deliberately delayed till it was late in the night. Meanwhile, the battalion commander called up on the radio, asking, 'Captain Singh, what's the progress? Over.'

'Sir, we have silenced one LMG, but there are more. I'm planning another attack after a few hours. Over.'

'Okay. Do you need more troops? One company is ready to be launched and the other two are held in reserve.'

'No, sir. More troops would warn the enemy and they would escape.'

'Roger. Keep me posted. Over.'

Twenty-six-year-old Capt. C.N. Singh from Dharamshala in Himachal Pradesh, son of Capt. Balwan Singh, wanted to go for the kill and send a message back to Pakistan that the Indian Army could not be messed with so easily.

A few minutes before midnight, Capt. C.N. Singh led fifteen of his best men and got within 50 feet of the enemy's second LMG post without being seen. Then, he signalled the other half of the company to give him covering fire.

As soon as the Garhwalis started to fire, Capt. C.N. Singh led a charge of his brave soldiers on the main enemy position, shouting the Garhwali war cry, '*Badri Vishal Lal ki jai* (victory to the sons of Lord Badri Nath).'

The enemy had not expected a daring attack like this and in the confusion, Capt. C.N. Singh succeeded in killing six enemy soldiers. The rest of them ran away, leaving behind their guns, ammunition and grenades.

As the Indian Army soldiers raised their arms in joy, their commander sat down heavily. His hands were pressed against his stomach and blood was oozing through his fingers. In the final moments of their charge, tragically, a burst of the enemy's LMG fire had hit the officer in the stomach.

Capt. Chander Narain Singh died a few minutes later. Once the account of his bravery was sent to Delhi, the martyred officer was awarded the Maha Vir Chakra (MVC) for his exceptional leadership, courage and devotion to duty.

Ayub Khan won Pakistan's first general elections in 1965, based on the recently adopted constitution. His opponent was Fatima Jinnah, the candidate of the combined opposition. He won but was accused of rigging the election as Ms Jinnah was considered extremely popular, a factor that became more evident during the campaign. Of the 80,000 people entitled to vote, Ayub got 49,952 votes, but even though all the polling booths were manned by the Army, Fatima Jinnah got 38,691. Thus began a period of general public mistrust and a decline in Ayub's political standing. However, public opinion before the elections was pro-Ayub, as per an editorial in the Pakistani daily *Dawn*. It stated, ' . . . Ayub has maintained a foreign policy that has raised our prestige high in the capitals of the world. He did this by normalising relations with China, initiating cooperation with the Soviets and trade with eastern Europe and by establishing closer relations with Muslim countries . . . Above all, the Kashmir issue, long dormant, has been reactivated.'

—*Capt. Amarinder Singh and Lt Gen. Tajindar Shergill, PVSM,* The Monsoon War: Young Officers Reminisce—1965 India–Pakistan War

7

NARIAN, NOWSHERA, KASHMIR, 7 AUGUST 1965

A military patrol apprehended two suspicious-looking individuals near Narian village, Nowshera, along the Tawi river at dusk. These disoriented and weather-beaten men, clearly not from Kashmir, provided misleading answers during initial interrogation, leaving the Army wondering about their identity. Subsequently, they were detained and transported to the local Army headquarters.

Under the cover of darkness, in a secure room, the interrogation commenced. The detainees, hands tied behind them, sat on chairs, facing an officer without any rank or name plate as per protocol. Silence prevailed as the officer demanded, 'Tell me the truth, who are you?'

Unyielding, the men kept silent, eyes downcast.

The officer signalled to a jawan, who left the cell and returned with a bag emitting a metallic sound. The detainees, anticipating the inevitable, looked up.

The officer reiterated, 'Before we proceed, I'm giving you a final chance. Who are you?'

One of them finally cracked. 'Sir, my name is Ghulam Hussain. I'm from the 8 Azad Kashmir Battalion.'

Pressing further, the officer asked for his rank, and the man hesitated before admitting, 'Captain.'

This revelation marked a significant discovery—the capture of a regular Pakistan Army officer on Indian soil.

The officer smiled and said sarcastically, 'Greetings from the Indian Army. And you?' He turned to the other.

The second man identified himself as 'Captain Mohammed Sajjad from 18 Azad Kashmir Battalion,' doubling the jackpot.

Now aware of their military affiliations, the officer inquired, 'Why are you here in India?'

They stayed silent.

The officer repeated, 'You are both officers. Out with the truth now.'

The two exchanged tired looks and after a few seconds, one of them said, 'We are part of Operation Gibraltar.'

The Indian officer frowned, 'Gibraltar? But Gibraltar is in Europe.'

They cast their eyes down and lowered their heads again.

Just as in the 1962 war with China, Indian intelligence agencies had failed to uncover any hint of this covert operation called Gibraltar.

The Pakistani officers thereafter shared detailed information, disclosing that 30,000 infiltrators were actively operating in Kashmir under Operation Gibraltar, primarily comprising individuals from Azad Kashmir led by regular Pakistani officers. As these infiltrators continued their strikes in Kashmir, the Nusrat force (named so by Bhutto after his wife) patrolled the CFL, preventing any potential Indian offensive.

This information swiftly reached the Army headquarters in Delhi, then went to the defence minister, Y.B. Chavan, and finally the Prime Minister, Lal Bahadur Shastri. The foremost concern among India's top military and political leaders was whether the information had arrived too late to thwart the unfolding Operation Gibraltar.

At the time of infiltration, the infiltrators were given seven days' cooked and uncooked rations. The cooked rations were in the form of chapatis, gur (jaggery) and shakkarparas. They were also issued false identity cards to facilitate local purchase of rations. Adequate money in Indian currency was provided to enable purchase of supplies from the locals in Jammu and Kashmir. Each company commander was given Rs 9000 to Rs 10,000. This enabled the infiltrators to subsist on local food supply for a long period. During the early days of the operations, the infiltrators paid for all their requirements, which were procured from local shops through pro-Pakistan elements. During the later part, however, they resorted to loot, arson and murder.

Command and control of the operations was exercised by the HQ, Gibraltar force in POK. For this purpose, an ANGRC-9 wireless set was provided to each force for long-range communications. A transistor set was also

provided down to the platoon level. Instructions and orders
to the infiltrators were transmitted from the Azad Kashmir
Radio in previously arranged codes at fixed times.

—'Official War History, 1965', History Division,
Ministry of Defence, Government of India

8

SHIMLA, PUNJAB (NOW HIMACHAL PRADESH), 8 AUGUST 1965

Lt Gen. Harbaksh Singh, the GOC-in-C of the Western Command, was at his headquarters in Shimla when the phone rang. He had been monitoring the Pakistani infiltrators' attacks in Kashmir and the ensuing responses from Indian Army units since 5 August 1965.

The situation was grave and escalating rapidly. It was undoubtedly one of the most challenging moments in Lt Gen. Harbaksh Singh's distinguished career.

He picked up the phone.

The ADC to the Army Chief, Gen. J.N. Chaudhuri, was on the line from New Delhi. 'Jai Hind, sir,' he greeted the Western Army Commander.

'Jai Hind.'

'Sir, the chief wants to meet you this afternoon in Jalandhar. He wants a detailed briefing on the Kashmir situation along with your command's action plan.'

'Okay.'

Lt Gen. Harbaksh Singh slowly set the phone down, his countenance reflecting the weight of deep contemplation. For the past three days, he had been receiving reports from Corps Commander Lt Gen. Katoch about relentless attacks on Indian Army and government installations throughout Kashmir. The arrest of two Pakistan Army officers near Nowshera had laid bare the sinister scheme of the Pakistani government.

It became apparent that Pakistan was engaging in a half-war, a strategy to annex Kashmir and unsettle the foundation of the Indian republic. In essence, Pakistan was executing a stealthy assault, attacking India from an unexpected and vulnerable rear.

Lt Gen. Harbaksh Singh grappled with the strategic implications, recognizing the urgent need to thwart this assault on India's integrity.

*

JALANDHAR, PUNJAB, 8 AUGUST 1965

The Army Chief, Gen. J.N. Chaudhuri, arrived in Jalandhar on 8 August 1965 for his scheduled visit to 16 Cavalry as the colonel of the regiment. The Air Force Chief, Air Marshal Arjan Singh, was also present that day as he was scheduled to conduct the inspection of Adampur Air Force station located in Jalandhar.

As soon as Lt Gen. Harbaksh Singh met Gen. J.N. Chaudhuri, the Army Chief asked, 'What exactly is happening in Kashmir, General Singh? I want a detailed briefing.'

'Yes, sir. Since 5 August, we have been receiving information about the presence of Pakistani infiltrators in Kashmir. They have entered our land and have spread out all over the state. We are trying to fight them as we speak, but the number seems to be very large.'

'Isn't that exactly what the Pakistanis did in 1947–48?'

'Yes, sir. But now, their number is even larger and, as you know, the Pakistan of 1965 is nothing like the Pakistan of 1947. The Americans have armed them to their teeth and they are getting restless.'

'Hmm . . . so they want Kashmir?'

'That's right, sir. Just yesterday, we caught two Pakistani officers belonging to two different battalions of what they call Azad Kashmir. These officers started to sing in no time and we now know exactly what their plan is. We had sent the message to you.'

'I know, I know . . .'

They were quiet for a few seconds.

The Army Chief then said, 'That this Ayub Khan, who has promoted himself to the rank of Field Marshal and calls himself the President, would turn out to be such a nasty character I had no clue. Did you know we were together in Sandhurst, UK, before 1947, when India and Pakistan were one? We were not just batchmates, but we were in the same platoon too . . . Anyway, what's your plan, General Singh?'

The Army Commander of the Western Command leaned forward, looked straight into his boss's eyes and said, 'Sir, we need to go on the offensive.'

The Chief was on his feet, 'Hold on to that thought, General. I'll be back in an hour. Let me get done with the basic purpose of my visit here.'

'Yes, sir.'

'When I return, I want to see your plan in detail.'

'Yes, sir.'

With that, Gen. J.N. Chaudhuri left for his planned interaction with the officers and jawans of 16 Cavalry.

A few minutes later, Lt Gen. Harbaksh Singh proceeded to the MES Inspection Bungalow. As soon as he had stepped inside the bungalow, the phone rang. The time was 6 p.m. and the Defence Secretary was on the line from Delhi.

'This is the Defence Secretary. Could I speak with General Chaudhuri?'

Lt Gen. Harbaksh Singh replied, 'Sir, this is Lieutenant General Harbaksh Singh, the Army Commander of the Western Command. The chief is not here right now. He is addressing the troops and will be back in an hour.'

The Secretary inhaled deeply and said, 'Gen. Harbaksh Singh, I don't think we have one hour. The Cabinet is meeting right now and a decision needs to be taken on this extraordinary request of the Jammu and Kashmir government that we have received.'

'What's their request, sir, if I may know?'

'Yes, of course. In fact, it's not a request, but an SOS call. They want the Indian Army to take over Kashmir to fight these infiltrators. They are saying the infiltrators have reached the outskirts of Srinagar and the situation is beyond their control.'

Lt Gen. Harbaksh Singh thought for a few seconds before replying, 'Sir, I don't think that is a good idea. If we hand Kashmir over to the Army, we will be playing straight into the hands of the Pakistanis. That is exactly what they want. Sir, the Army taking over Kashmir will send the wrong message to the local people. They will think we don't have control over the state. This will lead to rumours and Pakistan's propaganda will get more teeth.'

'Okay. Thank you, General.' The secretary disconnected the call.

Immediately after placing the phone down, Lt Gen. Harbaksh Singh called Lt Gen. K.S. Katoch in Srinagar, who was the Corps Commander of the Srinagar-based XV Corps. They had been speaking to each other three to four times a day since 5 August 1965 because of the volatile scenario.

'Gen. Katoch, how is the situation now?'

'Sir, it's grim, but under control. I'm waiting for 2/9 Gorkha Battalion to arrive, but more troops are urgently needed for Kashmir.'

'Right, let me give orders to airlift 2 Sikh Battalion from Ambala and head to Srinagar right away.'

'Yes, sir. I'm also thinking of getting some troops from the Leh sector.'

'Do that. But maintain an adequate number for the protection of Leh, in case China starts getting ideas. And, General Katoch, I'll be in Srinagar tomorrow morning to review the overall situation.'

'Yes, sir.'

After some time, Gen. J.N. Chaudhuri arrived at the MES Inspection Bungalow. He was accompanied by Air Marshal Arjan Singh.

Lt Gen. Harbaksh Singh briefed him about his conversation with the Defence Secretary and the reasons he had offered for why martial law should not be implemented in Kashmir. After that, he told the Chief about the urgent requirement of flying more troops into Kashmir.

Gen. J.N. Chaudhuri replied, 'I agree with you, General Singh, about not imposing Army rule. You did the right thing. About the movement of more troops, we have the Air Chief with us. Tell him what you need so that we can do it without wasting another second.'

'Yes, sir.'

As Lt Gen. Harbaksh Singh and Air Marshal Arjan Singh started to discuss specific airlift details, the Army Chief called up Y.B. Chavan, the defence minister, and conveyed that imposition of Army rule in Kashmir was something he did not recommend.

9

NAUGAM, DODA DISTRICT (NOW RAMBAN), KASHMIR, 13 AUGUST 1965

A contingent of Pakistani infiltrators approached the headquarters of the 8 Kumaon Battalion at around 5 a.m. on 13 August 1965. Nestled in Naugam, a quiet village on the fringes of the Pir Panjal range, this army compound was situated 200 km east of the CFL.

Despite the chilling temperature of 10 degrees Celsius, the soldiers manning the elevated sentry posts along the wired perimeter were alert and the three companies of the 8 Kumaon Battalion and the headquarters company maintained a well-distributed presence within the army compound.

As the infiltrators deliberated on their next move, a morning fog descended upon the area, reducing visibility to a mere 20 feet. Exploiting this cover, they emerged from hiding and began cutting the barbed wire between two sentry posts.

Preceding this infiltration, the adversaries had coerced a local villager into divulging information about the battalion's force disposition. Armed with the precise locations of Alpha, Bravo, Charlie, Delta and the headquarter companies, along with details about perimeter picquets, administrative structures, fuel and ammunition depots, the infiltrators were well-informed.

Numbering around a hundred, they were cognizant of the impossibility of defeating the entire battalion, boasting approximately 700 men. Consequently, the decision was made to target the commanding officer, creating chaos and facilitating their escape from Naugam.

The captain from the Pakistan Army, who was leading the infiltrators, handpicked thirty of his elite soldiers for this mission. At around 6 a.m., exploiting the cover provided by the fog, they penetrated the compound after cutting the barbed wire. Half an hour later, guided by their prior knowledge, they approached the commanding officer's room.

At 6 in the morning, Lt Col M.V. Gore, the commanding officer of the 8 Kumaon Battalion, was in his tin-roofed room, which served as both off-duty office and residence. Two jawans stood outside, keeping watch. Adjacent to the commanding officer's room were the quarters of the 2 i/c, while on the other side stood the commanding officer's Quick Reaction Team (QRT), armed sentries assigned to the personal protection of the commanding officer. The remaining companies and the main body of the command's company were dispersed across several hundred feet.

A sentry stationed outside the commanding officer's room heard a sound, prompting him to alert his partner.

Both raised their rifles, peering through the fog in the direction of the noise. Silence ensued for a few seconds, followed by another sound, akin to a boot crunching on the ground. Suspicion heightened.

Sentry One called out, '*Tham, kaun ata hai* (Stop, who is coming)?'

No reply was forthcoming, deviating from the expected response of '*dost* (friend)' and the sharing of the day's secret code word.

Tension escalated, and the next moment, a barrage of automatic gunfire erupted, targeting the sentries. Despite their attempts to seek cover, both were struck by multiple bullets.

Three actions occurred immediately in the face of the unfolding crisis. First, inside the CO's room, Lt Col M.V. Gore heard the sound of bullets. Recognizing that the enemy must have infiltrated the premises undetected, he swiftly withdrew his pistol, approached the door and peered outside, only to be met with an obscured view.

'Guard?' he called, but received no response. Proceeding cautiously, he ventured beyond the room, encountering the lifeless bodies of the two sentries. The security of his unit had been compromised, prompting him to take cover, as he surveyed the surroundings to his left and right.

Simultaneously, the 2 i/c, alerted by the gunfire, emerged from the adjacent room, marking the second prompt response to the situation. The third action involved the QRT, already mobilizing towards the origin of the automatic fire.

Anticipating the standard protocol, the infiltrators, well-versed in tactical manoeuvres, initiated a bold move to disrupt the Indian forces. Unleashing indiscriminate fire, they closed in on the CO, aiming to create chaos and confusion.

Despite the CO's retaliatory gunfire, the sheer numbers overwhelmed him. Realizing retreat was no longer viable, Lt Col M.V. Gore emerged from cover, engaging the approaching enemy directly. Some infiltrators were struck, but ultimately, the CO succumbed to a barrage of bullets.

With their mission accomplished, the infiltrators dispersed, leaving five casualties in their wake. Within moments, the 2 i/c and the QRT arrived simultaneously, discovering the wounded CO and the fallen sentries.

Recognizing the urgency of saving a life, the 2 i/c swiftly organized transportation, placing the CO in a vehicle and heading towards the hospital in a Jeep, with the QRT following in a three-tonner vehicle.

Not far from the cantonment, the infiltrators, anticipating this response, ambushed the Indians. Despite the odds, the Kumaonis fought valiantly, resulting in the killing of eight infiltrators before the enemy opted to scatter. The toll stood at five Indian soldiers and one officer lost, while the enemy escaped with thirteen dead.

The intended demoralization of the Indian forces, especially by targeting a senior Army officer, was the crux of Pakistan's strategy. However, contrary to expectations, the aftermath would reveal an unexpected resilience and determination among the Indian troops.

10

SHIMLA, PUNJAB (NOW HIMACHAL PRADESH), 13 AUGUST 1965

At the nerve centre of Western Command, Lt Gen. Harbaksh Singh occupied his desk, grappling with the news of the audacious attack on the 8 Kumaon Battalion in Naugam, which had culminated in the cold-blooded murder of Lt Col M.V. Gore by Pakistani infiltrators. The weight of the events bore heavily on him as he contemplated the implications.

Amid the turmoil, the ringing of his phone punctuated the air. It was his staff officer on the line.

'Sir, Major Megh Singh wants to meet you.'

'Right now?'

'Sir, he's saying he wants to meet you at your earliest convenience.'

Lt Gen. Harbaksh Singh, cognizant of the pressing matters at hand, acknowledged the urgency. Familiar with

Maj. Megh Singh, who was serving as General Staff Officer
(GSO) Grade Two at his command headquarters, he
imagined that the meeting likely pertained to the officer's
previously expressed intention to leave the Army.

Although Lt Gen. Harbaksh Singh had recommended
Maj. Megh Singh's exit, he sensed that the officer sought his
intervention to expedite the process in Delhi.

The fact was, Lt Gen. Harbaksh Singh had genuine
fondness for Maj. Megh Singh, harbouring regret over the
disciplinary measures imposed upon him during his tenure
at 3 Guards, his former unit. The repercussions of this
disciplinary action lingered, rendering Maj. Megh Singh
ineligible for promotion to the rank of Lt Col, consequently
dampening his enthusiasm to continue in the Indian Army.
The weight of this incident cast a shadow over the officer's
military career, influencing his decision to seek alternative
paths beyond the armed forces.

Accepting the inevitable interruption, Lt Gen. Harbaksh
Singh instructed, 'Okay, send him in.'

'Yes, sir.'

In a matter of seconds, a firm knock resonated through
the room.

'Come in.'

The door opened to reveal a broad-shouldered officer of
medium height. Maj. Megh Singh greeted Lt Gen. Harbaksh
Singh with 'Jai Hind, sir,' acknowledging the gravity of the
moment.

'Jai Hind, Major Megh Singh. You have to be quick.'

'Yes, sir.'

'Sit.'

As Maj. Megh Singh settled into a chair, the air was
charged with a seriousness that mirrored the urgency of the

situation. He began, 'Sir, we need to eliminate these Pakistani terrorists from Kashmir swiftly. We have already lost too many lives.'

The unexpected nature of Maj. Megh Singh's opening statement prompted Lt Gen. Harbaksh Singh to respond, 'XV Corps is doing all that it can, Major.'

'Sir, I have a proposal.'

'Go on.'

'Sir, I want to handpick jawans and infiltrate behind enemy lines to dismantle their operations.'

Leaning back in his chair, Lt Gen. Harbaksh Singh smiled and inquired, 'How do you propose to do this, Major?'

'Sir, I seek your approval. Once under my command, I will cause substantial damage. The Pakistanis will never dare plan such misadventures in the future.'

After a brief contemplation, the army commander said, 'Well, I appreciate your courage and initiative, Major. However, I believe you've served your nation admirably, and it's time for you to move on. Your application to leave the Army could be approved any day.'

'Sir, when I submitted the application, the circumstances were different. My country was secure. But now, the enemy is claiming the lives of our brothers and sisters. How can I abandon my nation in such dire times?'

Lt Gen. Harbaksh Singh scrutinized Maj. Megh Singh for a moment, the officer maintaining an unyielding gaze. Eventually, a twinkle of resolve sparkled in the army commander's eyes. 'Okay, difficult times demand difficult decisions. I approve this force under the overall direct command of XV Corps.'

'Sir, I promise I will not disappoint you.'

'I know. And I want to promise something too, Major.'

'Yes, sir?'

'If you succeed in your mission, I will personally pin the rank of Lieutenant Colonel on your shoulder.'

Pride swelled in Maj. Megh Singh's chest at the trust bestowed upon him by the flag officer.

Lt Gen. Harbaksh Singh queried, 'What would you like to call this force?'

'Sir, I would request you to name it.'

After a brief pause, the army commander proposed, 'Let's call it Meghdoot Force—the power of the clouds from the sky.'

A heartfelt smile broke across Maj. Megh Singh's face for the first time since his arrival. He rose, saluted and exited the office, ready to set his plan in motion. In the ensuing minutes, he initiated the selection of elite jawans from 3 Rajputana Rifles and 3 Rajput Battalions, based on his personal interactions with individual soldiers.

In the weeks to come, the Meghdoot Force would emerge as a formidable entity, playing a pivotal role in the unfolding battle.

I give below a comparison between India and Pakistan of the main teeth arms (armour, artillery and infantry) to show the relative strengths of the opposing forces just prior to the offensive.

TEETH ARMS	PAKISTAN	INDIA
Armour	352 Pattons	186 Centurions
	308 Shermans	332 Shermans
	96 Chaffees	90 AMX
TOTAL	**756**	**608**
ARTILLERY	72 X 105 mm Howitzer	66 X 3.7 in Howitzer
	234 X 25 pr / 105 mm Howitzer	450 X 25 pr
	126 X 155 Howitzer	96 X 5.5 in
		16 X 7.2 in
	48 X 155 mm gun / 8 in Howitzer	
	72 X 25 pr / 3.7 in Howitzer	
TOTAL	**552**	**628**
INFANTRY	16 x regular brigades	35 infantry brigades
	4 X POK brigades (18 battalions)	
	9000 Razakars	

The sophistication of the Patton tank was a byword in armour circles. In contrast, our most modern tank, the Centurion, was of World War II vintage; the Sherman, a discarded relic from the last world war, formed the bulk of our armour potential. The Pakistan artillery, most equipped with the latest American weapons, was a powerful factor to be reckoned with. Indeed, the shattering impact of Pakistan's medium and heavy artillery during the conflict tipped the scales in her favour in many an engagement.

It is evident from the above, that in terms of the numbers and quality of equipment, Pakistan had a definite edge over us in armour. In artillery, her superiority was decisive in heavy guns, while the quality of her mediums was far above our own. Pakistan, therefore, possessed a formidable combination of armour and artillery—a decisive factor both in offence and defence. Only in infantry did we enjoy a measure of numerical superiority. This was offset by the large number of hastily trained recruits. Moreover, the automatic and anti-tank firepower in the Pakistan infantry battalion was almost double compared to our own. It was assessing the human element that Pakistan failed.

— *Lt Gen. Harbaksh Singh, VrC (retd),*
War Despatches: Indo–Pak Conflict 1965

11

SRINAGAR, JAMMU AND KASHMIR, 14 AUGUST 1965

Lt Gen. Harbaksh Singh and Lt Gen. Kashmir Singh Katoch were in Srinagar on 14 August 1965, engaged in an activity that injected the atmosphere with solemnity. They had just presided over an intelligence meeting regarding the situation in Kashmir, and the gravity of the circumstances was palpable.

A move set in motion by Lt Gen. Harbaksh Singh, with the backing of the Army Chief a few days prior, was on the verge of realization. A new division, named the 'Sri Force Division', was poised for activation, its primary objective being the defence of Srinagar and the elimination of the enemy within the state. This decision marked the initial step towards gaining control over the complex ground situation.

Lt Gen. Katoch, in a candid exchange, expressed his concerns, stating, 'Sir, the news from all around is not good.

Except for their Kargil (Tariq) force, others are managing to inflict heavy casualties on the Indian Army and the state government's machinery.'

'I know,' replied Lt Gen. Singh.

Undeterred, Lt Gen. Katoch continued, 'The enemy is well-camouflaged and is mingling with the local people at will. In many locations, they have succeeded in terrorizing the locals into keeping their mouths shut too. We are like sitting ducks with the enemy popping up at times and locations of their choosing to strike from any direction. Liquidating 50,000-plus infiltrators by separating them from the locals is an impossible task for any army of the world, however committed and professional.'

'Fifty thousand is a bit of an overestimation by your intelligence boys, Gen. Katoch. I would put the number at 25,000. Look, the only way we can send the enemy on to the backfoot is by conducting an offensive action. That will not only make them insecure about their assets on their territory, but it will also disrupt the supply line of those operating on our land, making them disperse in panic.'

'Sir, I still think we must consolidate our forces within Kashmir first and focus on killing the enemies within. I also suspect that this war will go on for a long time, and we need to conserve our ammunition.'

'While I agree with the consolidation part, I think we need to shock them too. That's the only way we can get a handle on this situation. When we go on the offensive, it will puncture the enemy's confidence. Currently, both our divisions, 19 and 25, are trying to fight the enemy already on Kashmiri soil.'

'I have shared my views, sir, but you are the army commander, so we will go ahead with your plan.'

'We are going to begin by creating the Sri Force.'

'Yes, sir.'

The designated leader of the Sri Force, handpicked for the role, was Maj. Gen. Umrao Singh, the Chief Staff Officer (CSO) of the Western Command headquarters, directly under the command of Lt Gen. Harbaksh Singh.

A few hours later, once the activation of the Sri Force Division was complete, Lt Gen. Harbaksh Singh conveyed to Lt Gen. Katoch, 'Now, it's time for us to go on the offensive. If we capture the Haji Pir Pass and the entire Haji Pir bulge, we will effectively lock these infiltrators in Kashmir for General Umrao's boys to hunt them down. Also, with the pass with us, the infiltration from the enemy's side will stop.'

'That's right, sir, but the enemy is holding the pass in strength, and we don't have enough troops for such an audacious attack.'

'We have. Because they will not be expecting us to cross the CFL and enter their territory. We will do exactly that and take advantage of the shock. No further discussions on this, General Katoch. I will soon be issuing formal orders for your troops after the chief clears it.'

'Yes, sir.' Lt Gen. Katoch's response carried a tinge of resignation, acknowledging the audacity of the mission.

PART 3

CODE NAME: OPERATION BAKSHI

Capture of the Haji Pir Pass—attack from Uri (north side)

12

URI, JAMMU AND KASHMIR,
15 AUGUST 1965

At the headquarters of 1 Para Battalion, Maj. Ranjit Singh Dyal, the 2 i/c of the battalion, was conducting an operations briefing. All officers, including the commanding officer, were present in the SMR. The JCOs of the four companies (Alpha, Bravo, Charlie and Delta) were present too.

Maj. Ranjit Singh Dyal had a wooden stick in his hand. He asked, 'Sir, do I have your permission to start?'

Lt Col Prabjinder Singh, the commanding officer, replied, 'Before you begin, Major Dyal, I want to address the leaders of our battalion.'

Everyone stared back at him without emotion, as Maj. Dyal stepped to one side.

The CO started to speak, 'First of all, happy Independence Day to you once again. After the morning parade, we should have observed a holiday today, but the developments in our area won't let us rest. As you know, Pakistani infiltrators have entered the Valley and they are targeting the Army's and government's infrastructure. Since 5 August, many of our officers, JCOs, jawans and Kashmiri brethren have lost their lives. The infiltrators are also trying to shift the loyalties of the Kashmiri people, our brothers and sisters, to their side by spreading rumours. In doing so, however, from what I have been told, they are having little success.'

He paused, looked at the faces of all present one by one and continued, 'But when people are not following their orders, the Pakistanis are using the fear of guns, and it seems to be working in some pockets. The brigade commander spoke to me this morning. Though the formal orders have not yet been received, he feels we will be deployed across the CFL in the Haji Pir area soon. If these orders indeed come, it will be a god-sent opportunity for us and we will strike to kill. Clear?'

'Yes, sir!' everyone shouted back, eyes wide, jaws firm and backs straight.

The CO turned towards the 2 i/c and said, 'You may continue now, Major Dyal.'

Maj. Dyal stepped forward again and replied, 'Yes, sir. So, as the CO has said, we will strike to kill. Now, I know some of you are new in this area, but I have been here for the last three years. Let me give you an overview. To understand the peculiarity of the Haji Pir area, it is important to take a look at this sand model carefully.'

All eyes shifted to the sand model and he continued, 'As you can see, the town of Uri is located on the northern side of the bulge and the town of Poonch is located on the southern side of the bulge. Before 1947, a 41-kilometre-long road connected the towns of Uri and Poonch. The time required to travel in a vehicle from one town to the other at that time used to be around two hours. But, after Pakistan's unauthorized occupation of the area now known as POK and establishment of a CFL mediated by the UN, the entire bulge unfortunately came under Pakistan control. Consequently, the distance between Uri and Poonch is now 500 kilometres all the way via Jammu, and it takes more than a day to travel from one town to the other.'

All eyes scanned the sand model as Maj. Dyal continued, 'There's an interesting history attached to the Haji Pir Pass. It is believed that once, when Shahjahan, the fourth Mughal emperor who ruled the majority of the Indian subcontinent from 1628 to 1658, was crossing the area with his caravan on his way to Srinagar from Rawalpindi, he had a vision. In this vision, he saw a small *mazaar* (shrine) of a *pir* (saint). After waking up, he climbed up there and guess what he found.' He paused, smiled and continued, 'Yes, a mazaar that was exactly the way he had seen in his dreams. The emperor was believed to be the first person to pay his respects to the pir by tying a string on a tree there. Good, so far?'

Everyone nodded and Maj. Dyal continued, 'From history, let us come to hard facts now. The Haji Pir bulge has several peaks and our intelligence has confirmed that these are occupied by the enemy in platoon-size and company-size strengths. The pass itself is around 8 kilometres across the CFL in Pakistani territory. To capture these hill features will be a daunting task, but the only way we can reach the pass is by knocking down these tactically strong positions occupied by the enemy. We will have to go for the kill in a coordinated way, not just with our companies, but also with the other battalions of our brigade.'

After this, each and every peak, the *nallahs*, the contour lines, the approaches and other aspects of the terrain were discussed in detail. The officers and the JCOs also pitched in with their questions and comments.

The CO looked at the involvement of all the leaders under his command. He had no doubt that when the time came, the tigers of 1 Para Battalion would shatter the enemy to pieces.

Altaf Gauhar, a close civilian adviser to Ayub Khan in 1965, wrote several years later that the Pakistani military had initiated the conflicts of 1948 and 1965, as well as subsequent military confrontations, with India.

According to Gauhar, 'All these operations were conceived and launched on the basis of one assumption: that the Indians are too cowardly and ill-organized to offer any effective military response, which could pose a threat to Pakistan. Ayub Khan genuinely believed that "as a general rule Hindu morale would not stand more than a couple of hard blows at the right time and place".'

—Altaf Gauhar (civilian adviser to Field Marshal Mohammed Ayub Khan, President of Pakistan, in 1965), quoted in 'Four Wars, One Assumption', the Nation, 5 September 1999.

13

SRINAGAR, JAMMU AND KASHMIR, 16 AUGUST 1965

At the corps' headquarters, Lt Gen. Kashmir Singh Katoch was worried. Even with the creation of the Sri Force, the enemy was attacking the Army's and the state government's infrastructure at will. The XV Corps was fighting well, but the sheer number of the enemy foot soldiers was overwhelming. His intelligence assessment continued to indicate that almost 50,000 infiltrators had entered Indian territory and were using the local people for cover and provisions.

To make matters worse, the GOC-in-C had been insistent about crossing the border (CFL) for a strike. That would stretch his limited resources thinner, and it wouldn't be possible for the corps to maintain the supply line to such a spread-out terrain. The enemy was not in front of them, but was all around them. The infiltrators were also invisible, because they were not wearing combat uniforms but were wearing salwar kameez like the civilians. It was impossible to tell one from the other.

After a lot of thinking and deliberations with the officers at his corps headquarters, Lt Gen. Katoch decided to formally convey his apprehensions to his boss in the form of an official signal communication. He wanted to be sure that if things indeed went out of hand, as he suspected they would, this official signal would prove to everyone that he had put his foot down and had said *no* to crossing the border. Therefore, a short signal was prepared and communicated to the Army Commander, Lt Gen. Harbaksh Singh, in Shimla, with a copy marked to the Chief of Army Staff, Gen. J.N. Chaudhuri, in New Delhi.

When Lt Gen. Harbaksh Singh received the signal in Shimla, he was angry. The Corps Commander was challenging his military wisdom. This was tantamount to insubordination and therefore, he immediately called and discussed the matter with the Army Chief. The Army Chief gave him a go-ahead.

Consequently, the next morning, that is, on 17 August 1965, the command headquarters gave official orders to XV Corps to cross the CFL and capture the Haji Pir Pass. This was no longer a matter of discussions and deliberations. It was an order now.

With that, all Lt Gen. Katoch's reservations were put to rest and the XV Corps, like a well-oiled war machine, started to gear up for action.

According to the orders, XV Corps were to approach the Haji Pir bulge from two directions as a 'pincer attack'. From the north at Uri, acting as the upper claw, 19 Division was ordered to use 68 Brigade for the thrust. This operation was called 'Operation Bakshi'. From the south at Poonch, acting as the lower claw, 25 Division was ordered to use 93 Brigade for the thrust. This was called 'Operation Faulad'.

Curiously, the names of the brigade commanders tasked with the operation were similar sounding: Brig. Zoru Bakshi was in Uri while Brig. Zora Singh was in Poonch.

According to the order, the operations were to be launched no later than 25 August 1965.

14

BARAMULLA, JAMMU AND KASHMIR, 20 AUGUST 1965

Early in the morning on 20 August 1965, Brig. Zorawar Chand Bakshi and the commanding officers of the five battalions under his brigade moved in a convoy by road towards the 19 Infantry Division headquarters in Baramulla.

Zorawar Chand Bakshi was born on 21 October 1921 in Gulyana village in Rawalpindi district, located in present-day Pakistan. After graduating from Rawalpindi's Gordon College in 1942, he had joined the Indian Military Academy in Dehradun.

Commissioned in the Baloch regiment, he received an M-in-D (Mentioned-in-Dispatches) during the war against the Japanese in Burma in 1943, and a fast-track promotion to major due to his performance during World War II while stationed in Burma. After independence from the British, he was transferred to 5 Gorkha Rifles and soon after, in 1948, he was awarded the Vir Chakra during the first Kashmir war in 1947–48. In 1949, he won the MacGregor Memorial Medal, which was awarded for valuable military intelligence through reconnaissance, exploration, survey or other similar activities of national importance. In 1963, while on a United Nations mission in Congo in Africa, he was awarded the VSM (Vishisht Seva Medal) for distinguished military service.

By 1965, therefore, Brig. Zorawar Bakshi was one of the most decorated officers of his seniority who were on active duty. Known to be a thorough professional and affectionately called Zoru Bakshi, he was also tactful in handling personnel, both senior and junior, in the chain of command, an attribute which was to help him smoothen out not just operational matters, but also personal ones in the following months.

As soon as the convoy arrived at the Division headquarters in Baramulla, they were escorted straight to the conference room where a sand model had been prepared in meticulous detail the previous night by the brigade's intelligence soldiers. Maj. Gen. Swarup Singh Kalaan, the GOC, was already present there along with his GSOs.

Brig. Bakshi and the five COs saluted the division commander. He saluted them back.

Then Maj. Gen. Kalaan said, 'Zoru, let's start immediately. We don't have a moment to lose.'

'Yes, sir.'

Using a wooden pointer, Maj. Gen. Kalaan started, 'For the capture of the Haji Pir Pass, Brigadier Bakshi, you have five battalions: 1 Para, 19 Punjab, 4 Rajput, 4 Sikh Light Infantry and 6 J&K Rifles. I know these battalions were not under you until a few days ago. But all of them are present here now. How would you like to plan your operations? D-Day is 25 August. We have only five days to plan and execute this important mission.'

Brig. Bakshi replied, 'Sir, the battalion commanders are ready with their plans, and with your permission, before I sum up, they would like to present their plans.'

'Go ahead.'

In the SMR, the brigade commander, Brig. Bakshi, turned to look at the officers of his brigade and signalled with a nod. One by one, they presented their plans.

Finally, as the GOC looked on, Brig. Zorawar Bakshi took the wooden pointer from the last speaker and started, 'Sir, my brigade will mount a two-pronged attack. 1 Para will attack from the right, via the features called Sank, Sar and Ledwali Gali ridge, and 4 Rajput will pass through 1 Para at Ledwali Gali and capture the Haji Pir Pass. Meanwhile, from the left, 19 Punjab will attack via the Pathra-Bedori-Kuthnar-Kiran ridge and establish a link-up with Haji Pir.'

Maj. Gen. Kalaan asked, 'What about artillery support?'

'Sir, without good artillery support, it will be very difficult to dislodge the enemy from their tactically sound positions on the hills. And we need an experienced Arty OP (Artillery Observation Post Officer) who can guide the guns and mortars well. Unless the enemy positions are adequately softened, our attack will be vulnerable. Military intelligence has confirmed that the approaches to these heights have also been mined by the enemy.'

'Right. Don't worry, we have enough artillery. Our division has already earmarked them for you . . . We can give you 164 Field Regiment less one battery, 144 Mountain Battery, 39 Medium Regiment, 18 Field Battery and one section of 4.2-inch heavy mortar. Do you think this is enough?'

'Yes, sir. While it's great that 93 Brigade will attack from the Poonch side and establish a link-up with us at Kahuta bridge, our problems don't end there.'

'Elaborate.'

'Sir, what I mean is, after the forces from the north and the south side cut off the bulge, there will still be a few isolated posts on the east of the axis in enemy control.'

'Right, I'm planning to use 61 Brigade to neutralize these posts which are on the periphery of the bulge. And there is one more thing . . .'

'Yes, sir.'

'The army commander has approved the creation of a special operations force of almost a company size under Major Megh Singh. He's posted at the Western Command headquarters in Shimla and I'm sure all of you have heard of him. He's been allowed to handpick 100 men who will be acting like a mercenary force operating directly under the corps commander. Therefore, apart from 61 Brigade, we will also have this Meghdoot force to knock off the remaining enemy picquets.'

'Understood, sir.'

Everyone was quiet. The operational meeting was over and the stage was now set for the ORBAT (Order of Battle) and the countdown to D-Day, i.e., 25 August 1965.

On his return to the brigade headquarters in Uri, Brig. Bakshi ordered 1 Para to hand over the control of the nine border picquets under them to 4 Sikh LI Battalion and prepare to attack Haji Pir.

15

URI, 1 PARA HEADQUARTERS, JAMMU AND KASHMIR, 20 AUGUST 1965

The CO and the 2 i/c, Maj. Ranjit Singh Dyal, were seated together in the former's office when a jawan brought in the printed ORBAT.

The CO read it and glanced at the major. Then he extended the order towards his deputy.

'Major Dyal, I want a meeting with the O group in the conference room right now.'

'Yes, sir.' Maj. Dyal rose to his feet, saluted the CO and left.

Ten minutes later, there was a knock on the CO's door.

'Come in,' he thundered, his voice a few notches higher than usual in anticipation of the action that was to follow soon. After all, this was one of the most audacious attacks planned by the Indian Army, and 1 Para had been entrusted to do it.

It was the adjutant, Capt. J.S. Bindra, who saluted smartly and said, 'Sir, the O group is ready in the conference room.'

The CO got up and left the room, the adjutant following him. The conference room was at the end of the corridor. The door was already open. He stepped inside.

The officers and JCOs were seated. They jumped to their feet and greeted their CO in unison, 'Good morning, sir.'

'Good morning! We have received the ORBAT just now. Our battalion has been given the task of crossing the CFL and attacking the three features before we halt and let 4 Rajput Battalion cross us and capture the Haji Pir Pass.'

He waited for a few seconds for the orders to be absorbed before continuing, 'Our first task is to hand over the nine picquets we are presently manning to 4 Sikh Light Infantry Battalion as fast as possible and assemble at the AA (Assembly Area) by 24 August. The company commander of Alpha Company, Major Yadav, is on leave. Send orders to recall him right away.'

Maj. Dyal said, 'Sir, I would recommend we should not recall him yet. He is on leave on compassionate grounds since his mother is not well.'

The CO replied, 'Okay, Major Dyal. I agree with you, but now I need a volunteer to command the Alpha Company of the Sikhs.'

Maj. Ranjit Singh Dyal replied, 'Sir, I will command the Alpha Company. In fact, I recommend that I be allowed to command the Alpha and the Bravo Companies in the first phase of the attack. In any case, our company commanders have only two to three years of experience. They haven't seen any combat yet.'

The CO said, 'Major Dyal, I admire your fighting spirit even after nineteen years of service and I see your point about lack of experience as well. In fact, as the battle progresses, I will take on the responsibilities of the company commanders too.'

After that, a detailed plan was discussed and the meeting was over. It was also decided that the battalion would review its plan again before moving in for the attack on 24 August 1965.

16

RAJOURI, JAMMU AND KASHMIR, 24 AUGUST 1965

Lt Gen. Harbaksh Singh flew into Rajouri in an Indian Air Force helicopter on 24 August 1965 to oversee the final preparations of the 25 Division to attack the Haji Pir bulge from the Poonch side in the south. At the helipad, he was received by Maj. Gen. Amreek Singh, the GOC, 25 Division.

After the official salutes and exchange of pleasantries, the two flag-rank officers walked inside.

That day, Vice Chief of Army Staff Lt Gen. Paramasiva Prabhakar Kumaramangalam was also present in Rajouri.

After saluting the Vice Chief, Lt Gen. Harbaksh Singh turned towards the GOC and asked him, 'What's the latest position of your division?'

Maj. Gen. Amreek Singh gave him a detailed account of where his division's troops were located and ended by saying, 'Sir, we are constantly engaging the infiltrators and causing a lot of casualties among the enemy. But our own troops are perishing too. The attacks are relentless, as if the enemy has a limitless supply of soldiers.'

Lt Gen. Harbaksh Singh nodded and said, 'Yes, that's why we need to go on the offensive from tomorrow, D-Day.'

Maj. Gen. Amreek Singh hesitated before replying, 'Sir, we don't have enough troops to cross the border and attack tomorrow.'

'What?'

'Sir, I have taken permission from Corps Commander Lt Gen. Katoch, to not cross the CFL to attack Haji Pir bulge from the south side.'

Lt Gen. Harbaksh was wild with anger. 'Do you know what you are saying? This is direct defiance of my orders!'

'Sir, I don't have troops . . .'

'Call General Katoch right now on the telephone. I want to speak with him.'

Minutes later, Lt Gen. Harbaksh Singh was speaking to Lt Gen. Katoch. After giving him a piece of his mind, he turned towards Maj. Gen. Amreek Singh and said, 'If anyone disobeys my orders again, the consequences will not be good. I will not hesitate to deal with acts of disobedience in accordance with the powers vested in me by the government of India.'

Meanwhile, Lt Gen. Kumaramangalam was quietly observing the situation. Being senior to Lt Gen. Harbaksh Singh, both in service and in designation, he said, 'The plan of the army commander is an order approved by Delhi. It should be put into motion without any further delay.'

They were quiet for a few minutes.

Lt Gen. Harbaksh Singh studied the force disposition of 25 Division again and revised his orders, 'I want two companies of 3rd Rajput Rifles to attack the bulge from the Poonch side tomorrow. Order them to coordinate with 68 Brigade as they progress. After that, from 3 September, I want a full attack by 93 Brigade from the south side. Is that clear, General Amreek Singh?'

The GOC of 25 Division replied, 'Yes, sir.'

Lt Gen. Harbaksh Singh left Rajouri a worried man. The psychological warfare initiated by the enemy was turning out to be successful. Even the most senior commanders of the Indian Army, who had decades of experience, were crumbling. But he had more faith in the younger officers and the jawans.

To make sure no more lapses took place, Lt Gen. Harbaksh Singh therefore decided to micro-manage the operations himself. If there was one flag-rank officer in Kashmir on a day before the Haji Pir attack who was confident about the Indian forces, it was their army commander, Lt Gen. Harbaksh Singh.

17

FORWARD ASSEMBLY AREA, NEAR URI, JAMMU AND KASHMIR, 24 AUGUST 1965

Starting from Uri, the valley gradually ascended, reaching an altitude of 4400 feet and peaking at around 8652 feet at the Haji Pir Pass. On the other side of the pass, the valley descended towards Poonch along the Betar Nullah, reaching 3349 feet. The valley was surrounded by towering peaks within the Haji Pir bulge, with Bedori at 12,200 feet on the east and Bisali at 11,200 feet on the west.

In August, the entire area was vibrant with lush greenery, thanks to a robust monsoon in 1965. While the rains added to the beauty of the valley, they also created challenges for the Indian Army. The slippery and wet terrain made it difficult to advance. The enemy held the advantage, occupying tall peaks without needing to move from their bunkers.

After receiving their directives from the commanding officer of 1 Para, Maj. Ranjit Singh Dyal swiftly set his plan into motion. The determined leader mobilized his attack troops, consisting of Alpha, Bravo, Charlie and Delta Companies, and initiated their departure from the battalion headquarters in Uri.

The departure of troops was meticulously organized, with each company leaving in batches on foot to ensure coordinated and efficient movement. By 4 p.m. on 24 August 1965, all the troops had reached the designated Forward Assembly Area (FAA). This location, chosen by 1 Para Battalion, was situated within a dense jungle. The selection took into account the crucial factor of remaining outside the enemy's weapons range, a decision taken to mitigate the risk of exposure to hostile fire.

As the troops reached the FAA, they found themselves surrounded by the mystique of the jungle, a setting that added an extra layer of complexity to the mission. Nature, however, had its own plans, as it had been raining for the last few hours. The patter of raindrops accompanied the soldiers as they prepared for the challenges that lay ahead. The weather, while setting a stunning backdrop, also posed an additional challenge, making the ground slippery and shrouding everything in a misty veil.

By the time the troops reached the FAA, they were bone-tired as they had been marching for over six hours, yet their body movement was free and assured because they knew what to expect.

Despite the adverse weather conditions, the soldiers of 1 Para remained resolute, ready to face the challenges of the mission. Maj. Ranjit Singh Dyal, with his commitment to the mission's success, ensured that his troops were well-prepared, both mentally and physically, to navigate the terrain and execute their tasks with precision.

The battalion's plan, crafted in accordance with the orders, outlined a sequence of actions that, if executed with precision, promised success. The linchpin of the operation involved a coordinated effort by Alpha, Bravo, Charlie and Delta Companies.

The plan was to kick off with the movement of Charlie Company first, entrusted with the critical task of securing the Forming Up Place (FUP). Once that was secured, they would then escort Alpha Company for the attack. The command for this phase rested in the hands of Maj. Ranjit Singh Dyal.

Once Alpha Company was at the FUP, its task was to attack and capture the Sank feature from Pakistani forces. Thirty minutes after this offensive, Delta Company was to start moving ahead. Their mission was to cross the recently secured Sank feature and move forward to capture the Sar feature, situated 1000 yards ahead. If circumstances permitted, they were also tasked with capturing Ledwali Gali further ahead along this axis.

As Maj. Dyal prepared for the attack, he knew it was the last chance for the soldiers to enjoy a hot meal. The support staff had brought *degchis* of food to the FAA. Despite making every effort to provide the soldiers with warm meals before their attack, the limitations of the environment meant they couldn't heat or cook at the FAA, to prevent the smoke and light alerting the enemy. So the troops ate the warm meal as it was served, fuelling themselves for the mission ahead.

The other officers who had arrived at the FAA with Maj. Dyal were Maj. Patil, Maj. Rao, Maj. Arvinder Singh,

Capt. Naidu and Capt. Vaswani. Lt Col Prabjinder Singh, the commanding officer of 1 Para, along with Capt. Gurung, Capt. Bindra and others, were at the battalion headquarters in Uri to maintain operational, administrative and communication support with the attacking troops of 1 Para on the one hand, and with the brigade and division headquarters on the other.

By 6 p.m., the rain had subsided to a drizzle, bringing relief to the troops preparing for their mission. The officers sat on camp chairs placed among the trees on one side, creating a makeshift briefing area. In contrast, the soldiers rested on sheets spread out on the ground to protect themselves from the wet earth.

Aware that this was his last opportunity to address the troops, Maj. Dyal, as their leader, decided to inspire and motivate his troops, because once the battalion commenced its movement from the FAA towards the FUP, communication would be limited to signals, due to the need for stealth, to safeguard the mission's success.

Maj. Ranjit Singh Dyal rose from his camp chair, his demeanour reflecting the gravity of the operation. With a determined stride, he navigated through the assembled soldiers, reaching a spot roughly at the centre. As he came to a stop, his presence caught everyone's attention and a hush fell over the gathering.

In the ensuing silence, Maj. Dyal commenced addressing his troops, his words carrying the weight of leadership and purpose. He moved dynamically, turning as he spoke, ensuring that his gaze met the eyes of as many jawans as possible. The choice of his location and the fluidity of his movements fostered a connection with each soldier, emphasizing the nature of their mission.

As the drizzle continued, Maj. Dyal's voice echoed through the jungle clearing, painting a vivid picture of the challenges and triumphs that awaited them. The soldiers, seated in their groups, listened attentively, absorbing the words of their leader, their resolve strengthened by the shared commitment to the task at hand.

When Maj. Dyal started to speak, his voice was loud and unwavering, '*Dushman kayi hafton se hamari peeth mein chhura ghonp raha hai. Hindustan ki sarkar ne yeh rokne ka faisla kiya hai aur yeh bhi faisla kiya hai ki hum dushman ko Kashmir chheenne nahi denge. Mujhe iss baat ka garv hai ki 1 Para ko* border cross *karke us* pass *par kabza karne ki zimmedaari di gayi hai, jahan se woh Kashmir mein ghuste hain. Hamein hamaari kabliyat aur hamare* teamwork *ki wajah se chuna gaya hai. 1 Para ke bahadur jawano, hum Sikh, Dogra, Jat, aur Ahir jawanon ke dushman ko Haji Pir se utha kar phenkne ka samay aa gaya hai. Mujhe sau feesadi vishwas hai ki 1 Para zaroor kamyab hogi aur ek baar hum hamare dushman ka raasta rok dein, toh doosri* battalions *ke hamare bhai bache hue dushmanon ko dhoond-dhoond ke tab tak marange jab tak woh apne hathiyaar nahi daal dete. Koi shak?* (The enemy has been stabbing us in the back for weeks now. The government of India has decided to stop this and teach them a lesson for trying to snatch Kashmir away from us. I'm proud that 1 Para has been chosen to cross the border and capture the very pass that they are using to enter the Valley. We have been chosen because of what we are made of and what we can accomplish together as a team. Brave soldiers of 1 Para, the time has come for the Sikhs, Dogras, Jats and Ahirs to throw the enemy out of the Haji Pir Pass once and for all. I'm 100 per cent sure that 1 Para will succeed in achieving this objective and once we block this route, our brothers from the other battalions will hunt the enemy down in the valley until they are killed or they give up. Any doubt?)'

'*Nahin*, sahab,' everyone shouted back at him.

Then, in a more practical vein, he continued, '*Jawanon, apna apna* mess tin *nikalo aur khana le lo. Uske baad, paani pee kar, apni apni* bottles *bhi bhar lena. Hamare pass abhi teen ghanten hain.* Finally, *chalne se pehle humko apne* weapons *aur* ammunition check *karne zaroori hain* (Soldiers, take out your mess tins and collect your food. After that, drink water, and fill your bottles too. We have three hours. Finally, before we move, checking your weapons and ammunition is most important).'

18

FORWARD ASSEMBLY AREA, NEAR URI, JAMMU AND KASHMIR, 24 AUGUST 1965

After completing his address, Maj. Dyal threaded his way through his soldiers, smiling and nodding, throwing in an occasional one-liner joke.

The jawans of 1 Para admired Maj. Dyal. They admired him for his courage, for his honesty and for his leadership. Maj. Dyal had been with 1 Para for the last eight months and in all the operations they had jointly conducted, he had never failed to lead the jawans from the front.

Over the next one hour, the jawans ate their food. Once done, they washed their mess tins and kept them back into their *bada pithus*, filled water in their bottles and checked the readiness of their weapons and ammunition.

It was quiet now, the only sound was that of the falling rain. Visibility was around 30 feet.

After all movements had ceased and the senior JCOs of the companies had reported the readiness of the troops to their company commanders, Maj. Ranjit Singh Dyal once again stood in the centre to address his troops for the final time before moving towards the FUP and launching the attack on the Pakistanis.

He paused and looked at the faces of his brave and loyal jawans. Everyone was wide-eyed, alert and ready to go. But before giving the final order to move ahead, the major wanted to discuss the terrain. Awareness of the terrain and the *josh* of the soldiers had always been the two most important aspects of the winning side in any infantry battle.

Maj. Dyal asked, 'Who can tell us about the features of Sank?'

One jawan got up and replied, 'Sir, the altitude of Sank is 9591 feet and its top is 500 yards long and 200 yards wide.'

'Right! Sit down. Now, who can tell us about the terrain features of our area of operation?'

Another replied, 'Sir, while the top is bare, the slopes have wild shrubs and cedar trees. Also, there are two spurs on both the edges at the top. The one in the west is called Sawan Pathri, and the one in the east is called Kopra Lambawala.'

'Excellent! Who can tell me about the estimated enemy strength in Sank?' This time, Maj. Dyal pointed towards a jawan.

The jawan replied, 'Sir, according to our intelligence, it's held by one company of the 6th Azad Kashmir Battalion. It has Razakars embedded in it too.'

'Good. So who can tell me who Razakars are?'

Another soldier replied, 'Sir, Razakars are the tribal volunteers of Pakistan who are assisting the Army.'

Maj. Dyal smiled and said, 'So, they number around 110 and the total of our Alpha Company is similar. But we will have Charlie Company right behind us for support. That brings our total to 220, double their strength.'

Maj. Dyal turned to address the officers' group, 'Captain Naidu, a lot depends on you. As the Arty OP, I want you to direct accurate fire from our artillery.'

Addressed by his commander, Capt. M.D. Naidu replied, 'Sir, I will do my best. The artillery bombs will blast them before our forces set foot there to stamp them out in their final fight.'

'That's what we want to hear, Captain Naidu.'

Commissioned in the Artillery regiment on 27 September 1963, Capt. Naidu was yet to complete two years in the service. This was the first time he would be seeing action in the field and he was looking forward to it.

On that day, as all the soldiers sat in the rain, their combat dress soaking wet, water dripping from their rain capes, no one had a clue that Capt. Naidu's role would be one of the most important in this attack.

19

FORWARD ASSEMBLY AREA, NEAR URI, JAMMU AND KASHMIR, 24 AUGUST 1965

By 8 p.m. on 24 August 1965, the rain had intensified, rapidly filling the nullahs and making the ground even more treacherous. The temperature had dropped from 15 degrees Celsius during the day to 10 degrees Celsius, and at night, it fell from 8 to 2 degrees Celsius.

The battalion knew that the rain would make their uniforms heavier, slowing them down as they navigated the rain-soaked terrain with weapons and rations. The lack of sunlight due to overcast skies meant their clothes would remain wet and uncomfortable. Additionally, the rain threatened to turn their food soggy and inedible. The seemingly impossible task of capturing the enemy-held strongholds beyond the border became even more challenging in these weather conditions.

During the day, Maj. Dyal had spoken to Lt Col Prabjinder Singh several times to apprise him of the situation on ground.

Since the rain had persisted throughout the day, Brig. Bakshi too was regularly in touch with Lt Col Prabjinder Singh about the challenges of launching an attack on the enemy-held positions. When there was no improvement in the weather by late night, Brig. Bakshi called the division commander.

At that moment, Lt Gen. Harbaksh Singh had just arrived in Baramulla and was present at the division headquarters. Due to the initial hesitation from the corps commander, Lt Gen. Katoch, to cross the border and attack the Pakistani forces, and later from the GOC of 25 Division, Maj. Gen. Amreek Singh, Lt Gen. Harbaksh Singh wanted to personally ensure that the operation proceeded without further obstacles.

The inclement weather had added an extra layer of complexity to an already challenging scenario, necessitating the highest level of strategic monitoring.

Over the telephone, Brig. Bakshi informed Maj. Gen. Kalaan, 'Sir, I just concluded a conversation on the radio set with the commanding officer of 1 Para. Despite our companies being at the FAA, I believe an attack in this weather would be counterproductive.'

Maj. Gen. Kalaan inquired, 'What do you propose, Brigadier?'

'Sir, I suggest we delay the attack by twenty-four hours.'

'Wait, let me come back to you.'

Maj. Gen. Kalaan placed the phone down and briefed Lt Gen. Harbaksh Singh, 'Sir, the brigade commander has recommended a twenty-four-hour postponement due to heavy rains.'

Lt Gen. Harbaksh Singh turned to Maj. Gen. Kalaan and asked, 'And what is your recommendation, General?'

'Sir, I trust my officers in the field, and I believe we should wait it out for twenty-four hours.'

After a moment of contemplation, Lt Gen. Harbaksh Singh approved the one-day postponement of the attack.

* * *

Around 9 p.m., just half an hour before Maj. Dyal was scheduled to lead Alpha Company towards the FUP for the attack, the news reached the battalion—H-Hour had been postponed by twenty-four hours due to rain.

With no shelter, not even from the dripping trees, the troops now faced the prospect of enduring the next full day in biting cold conditions.

Understanding these challenges, Maj. Dyal gathered the JCOs and advised them to allow the jawans to take as much rest as possible. Guards were positioned along the perimeter of the FAA to ensure the security of the troops. However, due to the restrictions imposed by the proximity of the enemy, creating fires for warmth or to make tea or coffee was dangerous. Any smoke, during the day or night, risked exposing their position to the Pakistanis, leading to unwanted reinforcement by the opposing forces.

The night unfolded with soldiers finding whatever comfort they could amid the harsh conditions. The absence of shelter forced them to rely on their wet gear, and the biting cold added an extra challenge to their predicament. The guards maintained vigilance, scanning the surroundings for signs of movement or threat.

As dawn broke, there was no improvement in the weather. Maj. Dyal, in consultation with the JCOs, directed the troops to conserve energy and remain vigilant. The morning was spent in a state of preparedness, with the soldiers mentally and physically ready for the challenges that lay ahead. Discussions were held to reassess the conditions and formulate a readjusted plan for the attack.

By mid-morning, as the rain continued to fall, Maj. Dyal maintained a resolute stance. The decision was clear—despite the adversities, the battalion would hold its ground, awaiting further orders, and execute the attack with the surprise element intact. The soldiers, though weary from a night spent in these conditions, stood ready for any challenge, showcasing the resilience that defined their commitment to the mission.

20

FORWARD ASSEMBLY AREA, NEAR URI, JAMMU AND KASHMIR, 25 AUGUST 1965

At around 6 p.m., even though it hadn't stopped raining, the company received the signal for the attack.

With that, Charlie Company reached the FUP without being seen by the enemy and after securing it, sent guides led by CHM Mithu Ram to escort Alpha Company.

As scheduled, Havildar (Hav.) Mithu Ram, along with six jawans, arrived at the FAA at 9.30 p.m. on 25 August 1965.

He reported to Maj. Ranjit Singh Dyal, 'Sir, Charlie Company has secured the FUP.'

'Did you spot any movement of the Pakistanis at Sank?'

'Sir, we could faintly hear the enemy soldiers chatting. One person was singing for a while too. I'm certain the enemy has no idea of our presence.'

'Good.'

Maj. Dyal addressed the soldiers of Alpha Company for the last time, '*Sab dhyan do.* Charlie Company *wahan pahunch gayi hai. Dushman ko abhi hawa bhi nahi lagi hai. Woh sab aram se baithe hain kyunki unko pata hai ki hum* border cross *kar ke wahan tak nahin aa sakte. Lekin hamein bahut savdhani se aage badhna hai. Zara sa bhi shor hone se, dushman satark ho jayega aur apni* position *le lega. Woh unchai pe hain aur unko harane ka ek hi tareeka hai, aur woh hai* surprise. *Sab samajh gaye?* (Pay attention, everyone. Charlie Company has reached. The enemy has no idea that we have arrived. They are sitting easy, clueless, because they think we can't cross the border and reach their position. But we have to move ahead very carefully. If we make even the slightest of sounds, the enemy will become alert and take their positions. They are higher than us in position; there is only one way to defeat them and that is by surprising them. Do you understand?)'

Everyone nodded. No one opened their mouths, even though they were still at the FAA and here they could speak aloud. Maj. Dyal smiled. They were ready. But he had no clue that due to a few overconfident soldiers, they were going to lose their surprise in a few hours.

With Maj. Ranjit Singh Dyal in the lead, the jawans of Alpha Company started to follow CHM Mithu Ram and the jawans from Charlie Company who had been assigned guide duty for the passage from the FAA to the FUP.

The attacking company of Alpha was expected to arrive at the FUP by 10.30 p.m. and the orders were to attack immediately.

As they slowly made their way towards the FUP, the rain increased. The downpour was so heavy that it reduced the speed of their movement. The visibility dropped to just a few feet within minutes and the ground beneath their feet turned even more slippery. A few jawans slipped and fell, and others helped them to their feet before moving ahead. The jawans didn't stop. They knew that if rain was a disadvantage to them, it was a disadvantage to the enemy too.

The continuous rain and zero visibility, however, disoriented the guides of Charlie Company and consequently, for the whole night, Alpha Company went around in circles. Finally, at around 5.30 a.m., they found themselves right behind the enemy, deep in enemy territory and still 200 yards short of the feature's top.

Maj. Dyal had to decide his next course of action quickly. Soon, it would be daylight and the troops were already exhausted. The approach from this side was narrower and allowed only a few people to move side by side. Due to this, the company was in extended order with Maj. Dyal somewhere in the middle. It wasn't a tactically sound position for the soldiers to be in.

To make matters worse, it stopped raining and visibility improved suddenly. The Indians were about to be exposed in a relatively open space while the enemy was well-hidden in its secure position at a height.

21

SANK FEATURE, POK,
26 AUGUST 1965

At first light on 26 August 1965, when the Indians were still 100 yards short of the Pakistani position at Sank, the enemy spotted them and began to fire. The jawans of Alpha Company took shelter behind the tree trunks and rocks and started to respond indiscriminately.

Maj. Dyal shouted, 'Stop firing.'

But his order was drowned by the sound of the simultaneous firing of a dozen Indian weapons. Within minutes, the jawans who were at the front lines, facing the enemy, were left with just a few rounds. This was a disaster.

Once the ammunition was exhausted, the Indian jawans would be sitting ducks. Others couldn't go forward to help them due to the narrow approach. Once again, thinking quickly, and without any other option, Maj. Dyal ordered the troops of Alpha Company to conduct a bayonet strike.

Shouting the Sikh war cry '*Jo bole so nihal, sat sri akal*', the Sikh jawans charged forward, their bayonets in front of them. Maj. Dyal and others gave them covering fire from the rear, but the Indian soldiers couldn't get beyond the enemy's wired perimeter.

The enemy was succeeding in hitting the Indians easily. That's when Maj. Dyal called off the strike and the Indian jawans retreated, pulling their injured to safety as covering Indian fire continued.

Out of harm's way, Maj. Dyal did a quick number check. A total of thirteen Indian jawans had been injured, but one had been left behind and he had no idea about his fate. Extricating him was not possible now. The enemy knew about the Indians and was better prepared, with just a narrow approach leading to its position.

Maj. Dyal retreated along with the Alpha Company soldiers to a location below called the 'Firm Base'. This was too far for the enemy to cause any damage to them.

The first thing he did was to address the troops: '*Mere bahadur jawanon, aap sab ki bahaduri se hum dushman ke* wire perimeter *tak pahunch gaye the. Mujhe tum sab pe garv hai. Lekin aaj thodi kasar rah gayi. Hamara* attack late *ho gaya aur dushman ne humko dekh liya. Agli bar hum aur bahaduri se ladenge aur mujhe poora vishwas hai ki jeet hamari hi hogi* (My brave soldiers, because of your courage, we had reached the wire perimeter of the enemy. I'm proud of you. But we couldn't achieve our objective today. Our attack was delayed and the enemy spotted us. Next time, we will fight with more efficiency and bravery, and I'm confident that victory will be ours).'

Subsequently, Maj. Dyal embraced the injured jawans. In that poignant moment, as his arms wrapped around them, the expressions on their faces, initially contorted with pain, underwent a metamorphosis. Slowly, the pain-ridden features shifted, breaking into smiles that spoke volumes about the resilience and camaraderie among the soldiers. Gradually, those smiles transitioned into a taut, determined expression, conveying readiness to face whatever lay ahead. The silent exchange, captured in that shared embrace, became a testament to the unspoken bond and indomitable spirit of the soldiers.

The rain increased and again, visibility dropped to just a few feet.

The soldiers took out their Forward Field Dressing (FFD) kits and began to bandage each other. Leaving them alone, Maj. Dyal stepped a little way away and called up the CO, Lt Col Prabjinder Singh, on the radio set. 'Sir, the attack didn't succeed.'

'What happened, Major Dyal? How are our troops?'

'Thirteen are injured, sir, and one is missing. We had reached their wire perimeter, but the surprise was lost.'

'But why did you attack so late, Major? It's 6 a.m. The time of your attack was 10.30 p.m.'

Maj. Dyal took a deep breath and said, 'Sir, we got lost.'

'Lost? How, Major Dyal? This area should be known to us like the backs of our hands.'

'Sir, it was raining and the visibility was very poor. We trusted our guides from Charlie Company but they took us in circles.'

'Was it not Mithu Ram who was leading you?'

'Yes, sir, it was the CHM. But it was raining so heavily . . . even now, one can't see beyond a few feet. In the night, it was zero visibility.'

'Do you suspect any foul play, Major?'

'No sir. I trust our boys with my life. It's the weather. But I take the blame, sir.'

The CO was quiet for a few seconds and then he said, 'Okay, cancel the attack and return to the FAA. Let me brief the brigade commander. Await further orders.'

Maj. Dyal put the receiver of the radio set down and gave orders to the jawans of Alpha Company to retreat. The Sikh soldiers, tired and dejected, lifted their injured fellow soldiers and started to walk back to the FAA.

An hour and a half later, they reached the FAA. Leaving the jawans there, Maj. Ranjit Singh Dyal returned to the battalion headquarters in Uri.

This was the very first attack of the Indians across the CFL and he was expected to lead it. But he and his men had failed. As he travelled in the Jeep towards the battalion headquarters in Uri, Maj. Dyal was quietly outraged. He was frustrated too. But, as a mature and experienced soldier, he knew that winning and losing were part and parcel of his profession.

An hour later, when he entered Lt Col Prabjinder Singh's room, the commanding officer was on the telephone with the division headquarters. The officer he was speaking to was Lt Col Hardev Kler, GSO 1 (General Staff Officer).

'Yes, wait a minute, Major Dyal is here. He has just entered the room. Speak to him.'

The CO extended the phone towards Maj. Dyal.

Maj. Dyal had just saluted the CO. He now took the phone and said, 'Jai Hind, sir.'

'Jai Hind! What happened today, Major Dyal?'

'Sir, we got lost on the way and the attack got delayed. With that, the surprise element was lost because it was daybreak by then. Continuing the attack would have resulted in more casualties and beating the enemy was not possible because of the terrain advantage they had, so we had to stop and pull back.'

'Okay. So, what's the plan now?'

'Sir, I'm here to propose our next action.'

'And that is?'

'Sir, we want to attack again. I will request the CO to take the brigade's approval and from there it will come to you at the division. I have just one request—kindly get us the approval of the GOC. Tell him my troops and I won't disappoint him again.'

'I assure you, Major Dyal, the division commander will not stand in the way of your plan. Best wishes, Major. The division trusts your leadership and like always, we are proud of the jawans of 1 Para.'

'Thank you, sir.'

He put the phone down and looked at the CO.

The CO said, 'Okay, I have understood what has happened. Now, let us plan for our next action.'

'Sir, I want to attack tonight. But this time, there is no surprise element. The enemy already knows we will attack, so they will be ready. Therefore, we need the support of the artillery.'

'I had anticipated this, Major Dyal, and have therefore already sent for Major Keshri Singh, the battery commander of 164 Battery unit. He should be here soon.'

Just then there was a knock on the door.

'Come in,' thundered Lt Col Prabjinder Singh.

The door opened and Maj. Keshri Singh stepped in. He gave a smart salute to the CO and said, 'Good morning, sir.'

'Not a very good morning, Major Keshri. Thirteen of my boys are injured and one is missing.'

'Sorry to know that, sir.'

'Right, we want to attack the enemy again. Our early morning attack didn't succeed today. The enemy is in company strength and the approach is too narrow.'

'Sir, give me a chance. We will saturate the enemy positions with our 25-pounder bombs. When do you plan to attack?'

'Tonight, at 10.30 p.m.'

'We will bomb them for the whole day and right up to the time our troops attack them, sir.'

'I want well-guided and accurate firing, Major. Otherwise, our forces will just be walking into a hail of bullets.'

'Trust 164 Field Regiment, sir. I'll brief Captain Naidu, the Forward Observation Officer (FOO), and we will blast not just their bunkers but also their confidence.'

'Good.'

Both Maj. Keshri and Maj. Dyal saluted the CO and left.

22

FORWARD ASSEMBLY AREA, NEAR URI, JAMMU AND KASHMIR, 26 AUGUST 1965

From the battalion headquarters in Uri, Maj. Ranjit Singh Dyal returned to the FAA by afternoon.

For the whole day on 26 August 1965, 164 Battery kept on firing at the Pakistani positions on the Sank feature. Unseen by the enemy, along with his section, Capt. M.D. Naidu had moved very close to Sank. This was a crucial, though risky, step to provide them with adjustments for the trajectory angle of the bombs and resulting distance. As time progressed, Capt. Naidu kept fine-tuning his corrections. The firing continued during the night too.

At 8 p.m., Maj. Dyal received orders from the battalion headquarters to attack again. This time, he was ordered to lead

Bravo and Delta Companies. Alpha Company was to be left behind at the FAA and Charlie was to remain at the FUP.

By this time, just like the previous night, the soldiers had eaten their dinner, filled their water bottles and checked the state of their personal weapons and ammunition. There was a general calm all around. It had stopped raining too, though the ground was still slushy.

Maj. Dyal was sitting in a camp chair, as were other officers and JCOs. The jawans were sitting on sheets on the ground. They had removed their shoes and socks to dry them. It was cold and everyone was shivering. Most of them had taken out their blankets from their bada pithus and wrapped them around their bodies. Since their combat dresses were wet, the blankets didn't provide much warmth.

As soon as Maj. Dyal read the battalion's official order to attack, he got up and walked up to the Sikh jawans of Alpha Company, who were sitting in one group.

He took a deep breath and began to speak, 'Alpha Company *ke bahadur jawanon, mujhe aur* CO *sahab ko aap sab pe garv hai. Iss bar* Bravo *aur* Delta Companies *ko lekar jaane ka* order *aya hai.* Alpha Company *agle* order *ke liye* ready *rahegi. Kyunki Sank ke baad humko Sar aur Ledwali Gali bhi* capture *karna hai. Mujhe nahin pata main* Alpha *ko ek ghante baad ya ek din baad ya kitne din baad bulaunga.* Order *kabhi bhi aa sakta hai, isliye aap sab* ready *raho* (Brave soldiers of Alpha Company, the CO and I are proud of you. This time, the orders are for the Bravo and Delta Companies to proceed for the attack. Alpha Company will stay here and await their next order. Because after Sank, we have to capture Sar and Ledwali Gali too. I have no idea when I will call Alpha Company for the attack; it could be in one hour, one day or many days. Orders can come any time, so you should all be ready).'

The jawans of Alpha Company nodded. They understood the need to keep them rested for the time being.

After this, Maj. Dyal walked up to the Bravo and Delta Companies and addressed them, '*Mere bahadur jawanon, aap sab hamari* artillery *ki* firing *ki awaaz toh sun hi rahe ho. Jab tak hum dushman pe* attack *karenge, uske* confidence *ka* level *aadha hi bacha hoga. Lekin humko dushman ko kabhi bhi* underestimate *nahin karna chahiye* (My brave soldiers, I'm sure you have been hearing the sounds of our artillery firing. By the time we attack the enemy, their confidence will have been reduced by half. But we should never underestimate the enemy).'

He paused and then spoke again, this time louder, '*Kya hum taiyyar hain* (Are we ready)?'

The Dogra and Ahir jawans of Bravo and Delta Companies, respectively, shouted in unison, 'Yes, sir!'

At around 9.30 p.m., as soon as the guides of Charlie Company arrived from the FUP, Maj. Dyal led Bravo and Delta Companies on the attack. Bravo Company was headed by Maj. H. Patil and Delta Company was headed by Maj. Arvinder Singh. Although it had started to rain again, it was not as heavy as the previous day.

Maj. Dyal led Bravo and Delta Companies along with the two officers up to 100 metres short of the enemy position. Here they stopped and regrouped. No one could speak now. Capt. Naidu was still directing the firing on the enemy positions on Sank. The troops could see the bombs falling on top of the Sank feature and exploding loudly.

Maj. Dyal was in communication with Capt. Naidu on the radio set. Once everyone was ready, he ordered Capt. Naidu, 'Stop firing and confirm.'

'Wilco, sir.'

Everyone waited. Maj. Dyal knew Capt. Naidu would have to communicate the order to Maj. Keshri, who was commanding the guns at the base camp.

After a minute, Capt. Naidu's voice came back on the radio set and he said, 'Sir, firing has been stopped.'

'Roger and out.'

Their surroundings were deafeningly silent now. The time had come. But the Indians had no clue how much damage the enemy had sustained due to the Indian firing. Maybe they were well-entrenched in formidable bunkers and had suffered no damage at all. Or, maybe they hadn't bothered to prepare strong defence positions as they were well within the Pakistani border, and the Indian firing had decimated them.

There was no time to think. Any delay would give an opportunity to the enemy to regroup and devise a strategy. The time now was 10 p.m.

Leading them from the front, Maj. Dyal ordered the platoon commanders to attack Sank.

A total of around 180 jawans of the Bravo and Delta Companies started moving forward cautiously to attack the Sank feature. Ahead of them were Maj. Dyal, Maj. Patil, Maj. Arvinder Singh and Capt. Dhillon (B Company 2 i/c). The approach was narrow, so they walked in lines of two, their knees bent, all senses alert and weapons drawn with safety catch off, fingers on the trigger.

With each step, the Indians expected retaliatory fire. But there was none. Surely, the enemy had spotted the Indians and was waiting for them to get closer to inflict the maximum damage. It showed the enemy's confidence and an assurance of its control over the situation. The Indians were sweating, even though the temperature was around 10 degrees Celsius and all their clothes were soaked.

Maj. Dyal was the first to reach the enemy position. He took a cautious step on the flat ground. The place seemed to be deserted. It was too dark to make out anything. He moved forward, pausing at each step, his eyes scanning the surroundings. That's when Maj. Dyal heard faint music coming from one of the bunkers.

He changed his direction towards the sound, signalling simultaneously with his fingers to the soldiers who were following him to move in different directions. As he neared the bunker, the music got louder and louder.

So far, they had faced no resistance today. Had the enemy abandoned their position? This seemed to be the most logical explanation.

Maj. Dyal stood at the mouth of the bunker. The sound was very loud here. He looked inside. There was no one. It took the attacking Indians a few more minutes to realize that all the bunkers and trenches were empty.

In fact, they realized the enemy had deserted their post and escaped in such a hurry that their commander had left the radio on. As the Indian jawans walked on the treeless surface atop the Sank feature, they exulted.

The enemy had left behind many of their weapons too. Everyone knew that this meant they were now one step closer to their goal of capturing the Haji Pir Pass for India. This was the first Indian victory on enemy soil.

23

SANK FEATURE, POK,
27 AUGUST 1965

The jubilation among the Indian troops was cut short when, seconds later, they stumbled upon the lifeless body of Sepoy (Sep.) Lal Singh from Alpha Company, who had been reported missing the day before. Tragically, Sep. Lal Singh's body bore signs of torture, with his eyes gouged out.

It brought tears to the Indian soldiers' eyes. The enemy had not followed the protocols established for Prisoners of War (POWs). In the days to come, this was going to cost the Pakistanis, as it fuelled the Indians' anger many notches higher.

From the Sank feature, Maj. Dyal called the CO on the radio set and said, 'Jai Hind, sir, we have captured Sank.'

'That's good. Casualties?'

'None during this attempt, sir. The enemy had already run away when we arrived. I think they left in the final minutes before our approach as the radio of their commander was still on. But, sir, I have some bad news too.'

'Our missing jawan?'

'Yes, sir. He's gone. Torture marks.'

'Sorry to hear that. Message his name and I will inform his next of kin personally. And you send the body of our *shaheed* back to the battalion headquarters. We will organize his cremation with full honours.'

'Yes, sir. What's my next order?'

'You hold the Sank feature, in case the enemy reorganizes and attacks, and order Delta Company to move forward and capture the next feature, Sar.'

'Yes, sir.'

'And I have ordered Alpha Company to join you once again. They are on their way right now.'

'Yes, sir.'

Sar was approximately 1000 yards west of Sank, farther inside enemy territory. From the intelligence inputs available, it was being held by a platoon of around forty enemy soldiers.

After giving instructions to Bravo Company, Maj. Dyal addressed the jawans of Delta Company, '*Mere bahadur jawanon, dushman ki agli* post *ka naam Sar hai. Sar* feature *ke baare main kaun batayega?* (My brave soldiers of Delta Company, the name of the enemy's next position is Sar. Who will tell us more about the Sar feature?)'

One jawan replied, 'Sir, *Sar yahan se ek hazaar gaj paschim ki taraf hai* (Sir, Sar is 1000 yards west of here).'

'Good. *Ab* plan *pe dhyan do.* Major Arvinder Singh Delta Company *ko* lead *karenge. Hum subah jaldi* attack *karenge.*

Tab tak aap shakkarpare khaiye aur paani pee ke rest *kijiye* (Now, pay attention about the plan. Major Arvinder Singh will lead Delta Company. We will attack in two hours. Until then, eat shakkarparas, drink water and rest).'

24

SAR FEATURE, POK, 27 AUGUST 1965

At around 7 a.m. on 27 August 1965, Maj. Arvinder Singh began to lead the jawans of Delta Company towards Sar. There was sufficient light for them to see up to 50 metres. As they moved forward, visibility improved. There was no rain and the ground under their feet was a bit firmer.

Maj. Arvinder Singh was born on 20 May 1941 in Tharparkar district of the Sindh province of undivided India. After completing his schooling in Ludhiana, he enrolled in Government College, Ludhiana, for a year, before earning the honour of joining the National Defence Academy (NDA) in January 1958. Commissioned into the 1 Para of the Indian Army on 17 December 1961, it is noteworthy that, at the time of this pivotal engagement, Maj. Arvinder Singh had just three years and nine months of service to the nation.

Seven months prior to the war, Maj. Arvinder Singh had assumed the role of officer commanding (OC) of

Delta Company, which consisted of Ahirs. Recognizing their youthfulness and limited experience, Maj. Arvinder Singh, known for his athleticism and commitment to fitness, undertook the decision to rigorously train his company. His dedication and training regimen instilled a high level of confidence within his company, making them well-prepared for the challenges they would face in the upcoming battle.

As the Indians were advancing towards the Sar feature, they encountered two fallen Pakistani soldiers. An examination revealed the grim reality—these soldiers had sustained severe injuries during the Indian bombardment on Sank. Despite their attempts to escape, the gravity of their wounds and loss of blood prevented them from reaching safety, ultimately leading to their demise along the way. The sad part was that the enemy had decided to leave their martyred soldiers behind.

Maj. Arvinder Singh tasked the Indian jawans with a humane duty—to dig graves and bury the fallen Pakistani soldiers, ensuring they were spared the grim fate of being picked at by wild animals. In the stillness of that moment, with the air heavy with the weight of their responsibilities, a few jawans wielded their tools and excavated two graves in the earth. The enemy soldiers were gently laid to rest in these makeshift tombs, an acknowledgement of the shared humanity in the midst of conflict.

As the troops stood in solemn vigil, paying their respects to the fallen, the sun climbed higher in the sky, casting a comforting light over the scene. They began to move forward.

The Sar feature was visible as it lay around 500 yards ahead of them. The Indians slowed down as they moved, their senses extra alert now. The area looked silent and deserted from this distance.

But Maj. Arvinder Singh knew appearances could be deceptive. They could not take any chances as the Sar feature had not been pounded by the Indian artillery guns, as Sank had been.

As they reached the periphery of the Sar feature, Delta Company came under heavy fire from the enemy. It was a burst from several positions embedded well within the Sar feature.

The Indians took cover and Maj. Arvinder took stock of his men. Luckily, there were no casualties, in fact, no one was even injured. Further analysis proved that the enemy had actually not been able to hold their nerve long enough and had fired much earlier. It was a relief.

Protected in their positions, Maj. Arvinder had a brief discussion with the commanders of the platoons of Delta Company before ordering them to fire back.

It was a short but fierce encounter, after which the enemy soldiers decided to abandon their post and escape. This was unexpected, but the Indians were overjoyed. They had no idea if their superior ratio of men—3:1—had frightened the enemy, or the enemy was simply overwhelmed by the Indian soldiers' courage.

Courage, the Indian leaders understood, was not a virtue but a strategy, capable of transforming every soldier into a victor. Courage had only two outcomes: either the soldier would achieve martyrdom, upholding the sanctity of his motherland, or he would succeed in his mission. Therefore, the courageous never failed.

This perspective proved that courage, as a driving force, propelled every soldier beyond defeat. It gave them strength to face the enemy head-on, their commitment larger than themselves. The Indian leaders recognized that courage, when harnessed and nurtured, shaped destinies on the battlefield.

By 9 a.m. on 27 August 1965, Delta Company had captured the Sar feature. Everyone was smiling.

After posting sentries to guard the periphery of the feature, Maj. Arvinder Singh called Maj. Dyal on the radio: 'Sir, Sar has been captured.'

'That's excellent, Major.'

However, during consolidation after Delta Company had left, Maj. Dyal had realized that Sank was not fully secure, as two features called Sawan Pathri, which was 800 yards from Sank, and Agiwas, which was 1800 yards from it, were still held by the enemy.

As this needed immediate action, Maj. Dyal called Capt. Dhillon.

After Capt. Dhillon arrived, Maj. Dyal said, 'Captain, we are in enemy territory and they will do everything they can to retake Sank and Sar. Take your platoon of Bravo Company and secure Sawan Pathri and Agiwas.'

'Yes, sir.'

25

SANK FEATURE, POK, 27 AUGUST 1965

Maj. Dyal looked around the Sank feature now. The Bravo Company jawans had had a good rest during the night. The attack strategy had been working well so far. The only setback they had suffered had been the previous day, when their attack was delayed and the Indians had lost a precious life. It was now time to update the CO.

As he turned towards the radio operator, the operator extended the receiver towards Maj. Dyal and said, 'Sir, CO sahab is on the line.'

It looked like the CO had called Maj. Dyal first.

The CO asked, 'Status?'

'Sir, Major Arvinder Singh has captured Sar.'

'That's good, Major Dyal. Now, I want to move my command headquarters to Sank before you move further ahead.'

Maj. Dyal paused for a few moments and then said, 'Sir, I think you need to hold on in Uri for some more time. There are two features still held by the enemy near Sank and I need to push them back before this area is properly secure. Captain Dhillon is taking care of it as we speak.'

'Roger. I will wait.'

Capt. Dhillon had led a platoon of Bravo Company of Dogras to Sawan Pathri and captured it after a brief fight. After that, he moved to Agiwas and captured that after a brief fight too. By 10.30 a.m., both these features had been cleared of the enemy.

As soon as Maj. Dyal heard that, he contacted the CO again: 'Sir, we have pushed them back. Sank is safe now and the battalion headquarters can be shifted here.'

While Capt. Dhillon was on his way after capturing Sawan Pathri and Agiwas, Maj. Dyal contacted Maj. Arvinder Singh on the radio: 'Major Arvinder, what is the situation now? Any counter-attack?'

'We have secured the Sar area, sir. No counter-attack by the enemy so far.'

'Okay. Move ahead and capture Ledwali Gali.'

'Yes, sir.'

* * *

Maj. Arvinder Singh looked at his Delta Company troops. He was proud of them. His rigorous training had shaped them into a strong and cohesive force.

He started to move forward towards the Ledwali feature. As soon as they arrived at around 10 a.m. on 27 August

1965, they faced a fierce initial encounter. But once again, the enemy lost their nerve soon and ran away, leaving their weapons and ammunition behind.

With the capture of every feature, the Indians were penetrating deeper and deeper into the enemy territory. The Indians had by this time captured Sank, Sar and Ledwali Gali. The nearby enemy picquets had been cleared too.

26

LEDWALI GALI, POK, 27 AUGUST 1965

Maj. Ranjit Singh Dyal arrived at Ledwali Gali on 27 August 1965 at around noon along with the soldiers of Alpha Company a few hours after it was captured. Delta Company was already camping at Ledwali Gali.

Behind them, while Bravo Company moved forward to Sar, Charlie Company remained at Sank where Lt Col Prabjinder Singh had by now moved his battalion headquarters. The Indians were 5 miles (8 km) inside enemy territory. Everyone was charged and raring to go.

From Ledwali Gali, the Haji Pir Pass was just two miles as the crow flies. But the distance on foot would be much longer as it involved climbing down from the Ledwali feature, crossing the Haidrabad Nullah and climbing up again to the Haji Pir Pass.

Visibility had improved considerably and through his binoculars, Maj. Ranjit Singh Dyal could see the pass clearly.

He observed it for some time and found no movement. There could be only two reasons for this: either the enemy was hiding and staying out of sight, or the pass, which was deep in enemy territory, was lightly held.

Maj. Dyal lowered his binoculars and contacted the CO. He knew what to do next, but for that he needed the approval of the higher command.

He spoke to the CO on the radio, 'Sir, we have captured Ledwali Gali too.'

'Well done. Casualties?'

'None, sir. Like earlier, the enemy lost their nerve and ran away.'

'How is the weather and the state of the troops?'

'The sun is out now, so it is a bit better. The rain has stopped too, and from where I am, I can see the Haji Pir Pass through my binoculars clearly. It's just 8 or 9 kilometres on foot from where I am standing right now.'

'Roger. Can you see any movement, Major Dyal?'

'Sir, it's weird, but I see nothing. I think the Haji Pir Pass has either been abandoned too or it is being lightly held.'

'Are you sure?'

This was a difficult question to answer. Maj. Dyal, who could never lie to his boss, said, 'I'm not sure, sir.'

'What do you propose, Major? Would you like to first send a recce team?'

'No, sir. I want to attack and capture the Haji Pir Pass. Just need your approval.'

The CO was quiet for a few seconds before he replied, 'Without proper reconnaissance, it's too risky, Major. We might be walking into a trap.'

PROCLAMATION OF WAR OF LIBERATION

The Revolutionary Council of Kashmir proclaims:

Brave Kashmiris,

Arise, for now is the time.

We have suffered long enough under the oppressive and treacherous rule of impostors and enemy agents.

Long enough have we allowed the traitors, to further the enemy designs.

REMEMBER that a Hindu despot who ruled over us, in utter disregard of the wishes of the people, sold us to India in 1947. This was the second sale of our land through a fraudulent and ignoble deed which brought the might of the cursed Indian Army into our beautiful and peaceful land.

BETRAYED though we were, we fought the enemy on every inch of our sacred soil. And we should have won but for the intervention of the United Nations who obtained an undertaking from India that we will exercise our inalienable right of self-determination under a free and fair plebiscite.

The United Nations was duped and so was the whole world. India dishonoured her international pledge shamelessly and with utter contempt for world opinion.

She played for time to occupy our land. Since then every day that has passed has been a day of misery and every night a night of crime. You know what acts of cruelty, sacrifice and barbarity the enemy has been perpetrating under the shadow of guns and bayonets.

For years our great leaders SHEIK MOHAMMAD ABDULLAH and MIRZA AFZAL BEG have been languishing in Indian prisons but their determination to throw off the yoke of Indian imperialism remains unflagging.

We have seen our children butchered but every drop of their blood has illumined the path of our struggle.

Our women were dishonoured but in their agony they sanctified the course of our freedom.

Our brave fighters lost their lives but their dying calls stirred the hearts of their compatriots.

The will of our people remains unbroken: their united might unshaken.

The enemy is on the run. We will not rest content till we have chased him out of our land.

The time has come for us to deliver the final blow and hereby we take a solemn pledge to take up arms once again and continue the fight till:

(a) The usurpers are expelled out of our land;
(b) Our leaders now in jail are freed; and
(c) The will of the people is allowed to determine the future of our land.

The Revolutionary Council which consists of patriots of unimpeachable integrity and men of unswerving faith, has set up today the National Government of the People of JAMMU and KASHMIR which decree as here under:

FROM TODAY:

(a) All alleged treaties and agreements between the imperialist Government of India and Kashmir stand annulled and are no longer binding on us.

( )

XV CORPS OPERATIONS   73

(b) The National Government of JAMMU and KASHMIR formed by the Revolutionary Council of KASHMIR is the sole lawful authority in our land;

(c) Only the National Government will be legally competent to receive taxes and public dues from the people of the state;

(d) Any KASHMIR national who wilfully cooperates with the Indian Government or their puppet administration in occupied KASHMIR will be treated as traitor and dealt with as such;

(e) Every national of the state of JAMMU and KASHMIR who may be employed either by the Imperialist Indian Government or its puppet administration, in civil or military capacity, shall support the freedom movement of the Revolutionary Council in every possible way;

(f) The National Government will issue orders and decrees on the KASHMIR National Radio representing the 'Voice of KASHMIR';

(g) Any national of KASHMIR who impedes the freedom movement or disobeys any order or decree of the National Government will be dealt with as a traitor.

The Revolutionary Council appeals to the world to support this freedom movement.

Now is the time for countries who have pledged themselves to help all freedom movements against imperialism to come to our assistance.

We have nothing against the people of India but their Governments have established a record of treachery and dishonesty in the world. We expect all sane and freedom-loving elements in India and particularly the brave Sikhs, the South Indians and the Rajputs who have always given us moral support to lend us active assistance.

The people of Pakistan have stood by us in our fight. To our regret they have not done as much as we expected of them. Now is the time for them too to join us in our struggle for life and liberty.

Let the nations of the world remember that if we go down the light of freedom will be extinguished for ever.

And above all, you the people of KASHMIR, you are the ones who are on trial. You are the ones who must win this war for the sake of coming generations, for the sake of freedom and for the sake of the glory of your motherland.

Arise: now or there will be no tomorrow:

Issued by the Revolutionary Council of KASHMIR

SADI KASHMIR PRESS, SRINAGAR.

Declaration given to Pakistani
infiltrators by the Pakistan
government, page 1

Declaration given to Pakistani
infiltrators by the Pakistan
government, page 2

Haji Pir Pass

Brig. Zorawar Chand
Bakshi, PVSM, MVC,
VrC, VSM, briefing
Lt Gen. Harbaksh
Singh, VrC, at Haji Pir

Brig. Zorawar Chand Bakshi, PVSM, MVC, VrC, VSM,
at Haji Pir after its capture

Lt Gen. Ranjit Singh Dyal, PVSM, MVC, as a brigadier in his office

9 mm carbine carried by Maj. Ranjit Singh Dyal, PVSM, MVC,
during the Haji Pir attack

Lt Gen. Ranjit Singh Dyal, PVSM, MVC, as a brigadier with his wife, Mrs Barinder K. Dyal

Parveen Dyal, daughter of Lt Gen. Ranjit Singh Dyal, PVSM, MVC, with his portrait at her residence in Panchkula, Haryana in February 2024

2 Lt Arvinder Singh Baicher
in Agra in 1962

Brig. Arvinder Singh at
his residence in Noida in
January 2024

Credit: Author

Old newspaper clipping featuring
Lance Havildar Umrao Singh, VrC

Credit: Col (Dr) Andy Anil

Author with the son and grandson of
Lance Havildar Umrao Singh, VrC,
at Surjanwas village, Mahendragarh
district, Haryana in January 2024

Credit: Col (Dr) Andy Anil

Memorial of Lance Havildar Umrao Singh, VrC at Surjanwas village,
Mahendragarh district, Haryana

Col J.S. Bindra, adjutant, 1 Para, at his residence in Chandigarh in February 2024

Col Ranbir Singh, VrC, of 4 Rajput Battalion at his residence in Mohali, Punjab in February 2024

Col Surjit Singh Sandhu of 6 Dogra at his residence in February 2024 with the author

Lt Gen. M.A. Gurbaxani, PVSM, AVSM (retd), at his residence in Mumbai in January 2024

Lt Gen. M.A. Gurbaxani, PVSM, AVSM (retd) and author at the former's residence in Mumbai

'But if we delay, sir, the enemy, who now knows about our thrust on their territory, will get enough time to bring their reinforcements. After that, dislodging them will be nearly impossible. The time is *now*, sir.'

'I don't think I can take that decision, Major Dyal. We might just be butchered . . .'

'Or we might win, sir. *Ya te aapa shaheed, ya pher aapa Haji Pir* capture *kar ke* history *bana lange* (We will either be martyred, or we will capture Haji Pir and make history).'

Maj. Dyal, a Sikh, broke into Punjabi while speaking to another Sikh officer, his CO.

'I see your point, Major Dyal. I had heard so much about you, that you are a tiger. Now I know you are indeed,' the CO replied.

'Sir, *saadi charon* company *de bande* tiger *ne. Tussi sannu ek vaari* chance *toh de ke vekho* (Sir, all the men of all four companies are tigers. You just give us a chance and then see).'

The CO was quiet for a few seconds before he made up his mind. 'Roger, you start preparing for the attack, I will get the approval soon. Over and out.'

Maj. Dyal had a smile on his face now. He looked at Haji Pir again through his binoculars. There was still no movement.

27

URI, KASHMIR, 27 AUGUST 1965

Brig. Zorawar Chand Bakshi put the phone down at the headquarters of 68 Infantry Brigade.

He had just been asked by the CO of 1 Para to authorize the capture of the Haji Pir Pass.

The brigade commander didn't lose a second in calling a meeting of his officers in the conference room. The decision had to be taken in the minimum possible time.

Within five minutes, the brigade major called him to say, 'Sir, everyone is ready.'

'Okay.'

The brigade commander was on his feet and rushed to the conference room.

He waved his hand to cut greetings short. Then, gesturing with the wooden pointer towards the features on the sand model, he straightaway got to the point, 'The attack from the right led by Major Dyal is going well. 1 Para is just short of

Haji Pir and want us to authorize the attack and capture. But what I want to know is, where is 19 Punjab now?'

One officer got up and said, 'Sir, we have just learnt that 19 Punjab has failed to capture the Bedori feature.'

The brigade commander contemplated for a few minutes before he spoke next, 'The trouble with capturing Haji Pir is that if the enemy decides to counter-attack, we will have just one battalion there. Since 19 Punjab has failed, 4 Rajput must capture the Bedori feature for the move towards Haji Pir.'

'Yes, sir.'

'And what is the state of Operation Faulad by 93 Brigade from Poonch? Where are they? And by when will they establish a link-up from the Kahuta bridge side?'

'Sir, as per the report of 93 Brigade, they are way behind.'

'Haji Pir is within our reach and I am confident about Major Dyal and his boys. But we may not be able to hold on to Haji Pir for a long time if the other battalions don't arrive to consolidate our position in strength. I want everyone to give their views. Keep them very brief. I need to take a decision within the next five minutes at the most.'

The officers present expressed their points. The gist was, the Indians had to capture the Haji Pir Pass to deal a strategic and psychological blow to the Pakistanis and throw a spanner in their Operation Gibraltar mission, thereby trapping the infiltrators in Kashmir. This would make them go rudderless and the attacks on the Indian Army and civil infrastructure would stop.

Some more deliberations later, Brig. Bakshi had made up his mind and he approved the plan. He was taking a huge risk, because if it failed, not only would 1 Para be isolated deep inside enemy territory and get butchered, he would lose his job too.

Brig. Bakshi returned to his room and drafted his reply after some more thought. One fact was clear. Without a doubt, capturing the Haji Pir Pass would be a blow to the confidence of the Pakistani military. It would also send a message about the Indian resolve across all the enemy positions in POK, thereby giving the Indian troops an edge in future battles.

28

BEDORI FEATURE, POK,
27 AUGUST 1965

While 1 Para was facing challenges ascending the Sank approach, 19 Punjab, having secured Ring Contour NM 1903 and Pathra feature, had confronted the formidable Bedori Hill. Bedori was the highest hill feature in the entire Haji Pir bulge, towering at over 12,200 feet.

Despite a determined assault by the battalion, the Pakistani forces held their ground, displaying stubborn resistance. They had successfully repelled the advance of 19 Punjab, compelling them to retreat to their firm base.

Following this setback, 7 Bihar Battalion was deployed to attack the post, but once again, the Bedori feature resisted capture. This was followed by an additional attempt by 4 Rajput Battalion after one day, but the feature couldn't be captured.

This development dealt a significant blow to the objectives of 68 Brigade. Despite 1 Para's successful advancement, nearly reaching the Haji Pir Pass after securing three crucial features in enemy territory, the progress of the 19 Punjab and 4 Rajput Battalions was hindered, with their movement halted at Bedori Hill from the opposite direction. The situation resulted in a stalemate, halting further progress.

According to Indian intelligence reports, Bedori was under a platoon from the 6 Azad Kashmir Battalion. Despite facing three successive attacks from Indian battalions over the course of three days, the defenders held their ground. While acknowledging their resilience, the Indians recognized the urgent need to act.

That's when the commanding officer of 19 Punjab, Lt Col Sampuran Singh, called Brig. Zorawar Chand Bakshi on the radio: 'Good morning, sir.'

'Good morning, Colonel Sampuran Singh.'

'Sir, I want to make another attempt to capture Bedori.'

'Are you sure? 4 Rajput and 7 Bihar also tried after your first attempt failed.'

'Sir, the boys are ready. We will be using the approach from the east side this time. It will work.'

'All the best, Colonel.'

Fuelled by determination and incensed by their previous failure, the Punjabis launched a fierce assault from the east, and this time, nothing could impede their success.

On the night of 28 August, 19 Punjab shifted their focus eastward, crossing the CFL near Gagarhil and advancing up the Dothalian Nullah towards Bedori.

Ascending the Bedori spur, they launched an assault and successfully seized control of the feature by 6 a.m. on

29 August. However, upon reaching the position, they discovered that the enemy had retreated. One possible reason for the abandonment of the location could have been the news of the Indian forces' advance towards Haji Pir.

Both Bedori and Kuthanar di Gali NR 1799 were conquered on 29 August 1965. Later, Lt Col Sampuran Singh was awarded the Vir Chakra for his bravery and leadership.

29

LEDWALI FEATURE,
POK (ACROSS CFL), 27 AUGUST 1965

We rewind the story here by two days. At Ledwali Gali feature, Maj. Ranjit Singh Dyal was pacing relentlessly, his anxiety palpable as he awaited the crucial approval to launch an attack on the Haji Pir Pass.

In the intricate web of military bureaucracy, every ticking second felt like a precious grain of sand slipping away. The jawans, the JCOs and the officers, all stood poised and ready. All that was needed was the official order to go ahead.

Earlier in the day, anticipating the need to secure strategic positions, Maj. Dyal had dispatched Charlie Company, led by Maj. Rao, to capture Point 10033, which the company successfully occupied after finding it abandoned by the enemy.

Finally, at around 3 p.m., the long-awaited approval arrived, marking the end of the four hours that had felt like an eternity to Maj. Dyal and the valiant soldiers of 1 Para. The bureaucratic process, though swift on paper, carried with it the weight of urgency that only those on the front lines could truly comprehend.

With the green light signalling the commencement of the operation, Maj. Dyal and his troops sprang into action. Selecting the most capable soldiers from Alpha and Delta Companies, Maj. Dyal formed an assorted company to spearhead the advance with the objective of attacking and capturing the Haji Pir Pass.

Those who had sustained injuries were left behind at Ledwali Gali under the capable leadership of Maj. Arvinder Singh, ensuring that they received the necessary care while the rest of the unit pressed forward towards their mission.

Within half an hour, Maj. Dyal and his soldiers started to move down along the slope towards Haidrabad Nullah, situated just below them towards the west. Maj. Dyal was also accompanied by Capt. Vaswani, the officer in charge of the mortar platoon.

However, their journey was met with an unexpected hindrance. The heavens unleashed a torrential downpour once again, as if the gods themselves sought to impede the progress of the Indian forces. The rain, sudden and intense, transformed the terrain into a slippery quagmire, and visibility plummeted to near zero, adding another challenge to their mission.

The heavy rain significantly slowed down Maj. Dyal and his troops. Despite taking all precautions, the jawans struggled, slipping and sliding down the slope, each step fraught with the risk of injury.

The Haidrabad Nullah, coursing its way between the Ledwali feature and the Haji Pir Pass, became a formidable obstacle. By the time the troops reached this water body, the clock had ticked to 5 p.m. The nullah's altitude stood at 6430 feet, while the Haji Pir Pass loomed above at 8530 feet.

A daunting ascent of 2100 feet now lay in front of the Indian forces as they faced the challenge of climbing towards their target amid the relentless rain and the unforgiving landscape.

As the rain continued its assault and visibility remained near zero, Maj. Dyal found himself thrust into an unexpected and hostile situation. Before he could chart his next move, the echoes of gunfire erupted, signalling an imminent threat. A barrage from an MMG and 81 mm mortar assaulted them, revealing that the enemy had spotted them despite the weather conditions.

Swiftly taking cover, the Indian forces braced themselves for the onslaught. However, a new challenge emerged as they faced a barrage of gunfire from another direction, this time originating from the retreating Razakars. These Pathans, having abandoned their posts at Sawan Pathri and Agiwas after a brief skirmish with Capt. Dhillon and his troops of Bravo Company, now posed an additional threat to Maj. Dyal's advancing troops.

The situation demanded decisive action. The Razakars, predominantly Pathans, needed to be neutralized to allow Maj. Dyal and his forces to maintain their momentum towards Haji Pir without further hindrance.

Recognizing the gravity of the moment, Maj. Dyal summoned Subedar (Sub.) Arjun Singh, the stalwart platoon commander of the 11 Platoon of Delta Company, and conveyed his instructions.

'Subedar Arjun, take your platoon and dislodge those Pathans from their position. I want you to make them pay for their misadventure.'

'Ji, sahab. Platoon 11 is prepared to handle them. Leave them to us, and you continue towards Haji Pir.'

'Your platoon can join us from the rear if your operation is swift. However, if it takes longer, you have the option to return to Ledwali Gali.'

'Ji, sahab,' Sub. Arjun acknowledged, his assurance resonating with his commitment to execute the mission at hand. The exchange embodied the coordination and clarity that characterized Maj. Dyal's leadership in the face of unexpected challenges on the path towards Haji Pir.

Sub. Arjun saluted and left. Within seconds, he was addressing his platoon of thirty-five Ahirs. Once done, the 11 platoon of Delta Company began to make their way towards the location of the Razakars.

Meanwhile, Maj. Dyal's attack party comprising the remaining soldiers of Alpha and Delta Companies decided to cross the nullah on their way to the Haji Pir Pass. Undeterred by the relentless rain, they waded through the waist-high water of the Haidrabad Nullah, each step a struggle against the fast-moving current. Since they were carrying extra rations, blankets, communication sets, weapons and ammunition, the crossing proved to be a challenge.

By the time the Indian officers and jawans reached the other side of the Haidrabad Nullah, the sun had set, shrouding the mountainous terrain in darkness. The urgency of their mission left no time to send guides ahead to navigate the unfamiliar territory. The mountain before them presented an ominous silhouette against the fading light, with no path marked on the maps they carried.

As they began their ascent in the diminishing light, the absence of a marked trail became evident. Within minutes, darkness enveloped them, making navigation treacherous. Maj. Dyal, leading the way, guided the officers and jawans through the uncharted territory.

In the hushed and uncertain night, a faint whiff of smoke caught Maj. Dyal's attention. He raised his hand, signalling for the group to halt, which prompted everyone to freeze in their tracks.

The distinct scent lingered in the air, intriguing and mysterious. It was clear that they were still a considerable distance from the pass, ruling out the possibility of the smoke emanating from the enemy soldiers' langar at the Haji Pir Pass.

Cautiously, Maj. Dyal and his troops moved forward, following the smell of smoke. Soon, they stumbled upon the source—a solitary hut with smoke curling from its chimney. Surrounded by darkness, the hut stood alone, with no other structures in the vicinity.

Wary of potential threats, Maj. Dyal dispatched two patrols to scout the surrounding area while the rest of the group maintained a vigilant stance, weapons at ready position. Five minutes later, the patrols returned with the report that no other huts or signs of people were found nearby.

The mystery deepened—who could be inside the hut? Were they innocent villagers seeking refuge from the weather? Or perhaps enemy soldiers strategically using it as a picquet? The possibilities loomed large, heightening the tension as Maj. Dyal contemplated how to approach the hut.

30

HAIDRABAD NULLAH, POK (ACROSS CFL), 27 AUGUST 1965

Leaving the main body of his troops behind, Maj. Dyal, accompanied by a select dozen soldiers, advanced towards the solitary hut. Their guns aimed at the door from all angles, they approached the structure with the tension of an imminent encounter.

With a hard kick, Maj. Dyal broke the door open, revealing a startling scene inside.

Around ten men were huddled together, their figures outlined by the flickering flames of a fire in the centre. Startled by the sudden intrusion, the men looked up to find themselves staring down the barrels of a dozen guns, each weapon trained on their faces.

Maj. Dyal asked sternly, 'Who are you?'

One among them, appearing to be their leader, responded, 'Sir, we are from the post on the CFL opposite Uri.'

Aware of the posts located on a height opposite Uri just across the CFL, Maj. Dyal pressed further, 'What are you doing here?'

The leader explained, 'Sir, we are on our way to Muzaffarabad after our tenure. We were relieved from our post yesterday.'

Observing that they were unarmed, Maj. Dyal, considering the normal practice of leaving weapons at the post, felt a momentary relief. Recognizing a potential opportunity, he inquired, 'Are you people Kashmiri?'

'No, sir, we are Pathan.'

Ordering his men to tie them up, Maj. Dyal remained cautious. The leader appealed, 'Sir, there is no need to tie us. We mean you no harm.'

Maj. Dyal countered sharply, 'Wrong. If you don't intend us any harm, why were you manning that post on the border?'

The man remained silent.

Pressing further, Maj. Dyal interrogated, 'Why were you firing on our positions at Rustom post and others from time to time?'

After a hesitant pause, the man admitted, 'For money, sir. We are very poor. The Pakistan government came to our village and said they would give us money if we manned the border posts.'

'And they instructed you to fire at us?' Maj. Dyal probed.

The leader nodded, and Maj. Dyal scrutinized the impoverished, weather-worn faces before him. It seemed the Pakistani leadership's motivations had fallen short. These men, Maj. Dyal reckoned, could prove useful.

Leaving his armed guards behind, Maj. Dyal huddled with Capt. Vaswani and his JCOs. He asked, 'Are you thinking what I'm thinking?' They nodded in agreement.

Returning to the captured men, Maj. Dyal declared, 'We will not harm you if you help us reach Haji Pir. But the question is, how can you help?'

The leader promptly responded, 'Sir, we can lift your loads.'

A subtle smile played on Maj. Dyal's lips as he nodded in approval. Soon, the Pathans were entrusted with the burdensome communication sets, spare batteries, ammunition bags and other heavy items. With armed jawans herding them by the movement of their muzzles from right behind them and the sides, the enemy soldiers started to climb as part of the Indian attacking force.

As if in defiance of their advance, the rain intensified, transforming the already challenging terrain into a quagmire of mud and slippery slopes. The downpour caused the top layer of clay to be washed away, rendering each step risky. The conditions claimed their toll, with every few seconds marked by the sound of someone slipping on the surface.

Realizing the futility of traversing the slippery landscape while upright, the troops were compelled to abandon walking altogether. In a desperate attempt to maintain progress, they started crawling on all fours. This mode of movement not only added to the physical strain but also reduced their speed.

By 2.30 a.m., the soldiers found themselves far from their destination of Haji Pir. Maj. Dyal, relying on his intuition, estimated that they were only halfway.

The rain and the landscape had slowed their advance, testing the mettle of the Indian forces as they persevered in pursuit of their mission.

31

HAJI PIR PASS, POK, 28 AUGUST 1965

Undeterred by the challenges posed by the weather and terrain, Maj. Dyal and his soldiers pressed on towards their target. Fully aware that movement was their ally, Maj. Dyal urged his men forward, demonstrating an unwavering commitment to the mission. The rain seemed to be no match for their resolve.

At 4.30 a.m. on 28 August 1965, recognizing the need for caution, Maj. Dyal ordered a temporary halt. Sending out a patrol to scout the path ahead, he prioritized the safety of his men. As the patrol ventured into the dark expanse, Maj. Dyal addressed the fatigued soldiers, '*Ab hum kuch* time *ke liye aaram karenge. Shakkarpare khao aur paani piyo. Ek ghante ke baad aage badhenge* (Now, I want you to rest for some time. Eat your shakkarparas, drink your water. We will move ahead after one hour).'

While the soldiers rested and nourished themselves, the patrol returned half an hour later with positive news—no signs of any obstacle ahead.

Maj. Dyal inquired, 'Did you see anything?'

The patrol leader responded, 'Sir, we saw nothing.'

Seizing the brief respite, Maj. Dyal found a moment to reflect. This was the juncture where history hung in the balance—whether they succeeded in capturing the pass, whether they emerged from this ordeal alive, it was a pivotal moment in time. Trusting the capabilities of each soldier in his company, particularly the Sikh jawans of Alpha Company and the Ahir jawans of Delta Company, Maj. Dyal felt assured of their mettle. Renowned for their prowess in sports, athletics, kabaddi, boxing and tug-of-war, these soldiers embodied excellence.

The Indian troops resumed their march at 5.30 a.m., entering the realm of dawn, yet with no sight of the elusive Haji Pir Pass. As daylight filtered through the trees, their pace quickened, shedding the previous necessity of crawling on all fours. Confidence replaced the earlier apprehension, even as rain continued to fall.

By 8 a.m., Alpha and Delta Companies were within 100 metres of the target. Maj. Dyal called for a pause, realizing the need to finalize the attack strategy. Three crucial elements occupied his considerations: attacking from a position of elevation, keeping artillery on standby if necessary and designating a platoon for covering fire.

Addressing Capt. Vaswani, Maj. Dyal said, 'Captain Vaswani, you stay here with a platoon and give us covering fire. Okay?'

'Yes, sir,' replied Capt. Vaswani.

Satisfied with the understanding, Maj. Dyal led one platoon to approach the right shoulder of the pass. Descending below it, he ascended the shoulder and surveyed the area—no signs of resistance were apparent.

The Indians thereafter descended into the pass, only to find it eerily abandoned. The time was 10 a.m., and the rain had finally ceased. The enemy had relinquished the Haji Pir Pass, leaving it unguarded.

A wave of elation swept through the exhausted Indian soldiers. After three days of marches, crawling through hostile terrain, engaging in combat and pressing on with minimal sleep and sustenance, they had achieved the unthinkable— capturing Pakistan's strategic position 8 kilometres within its territory.

Tears of joy flowed as the fatigued soldiers embraced each other in congratulations. The news of their determination and patriotism had instilled fear in the hearts of the Pakistani soldiers, compelling them to abandon their post, leaving behind weapons and ammunition.

The triumphant Indians had captured the Haji Pir Pass, marking the culmination of an extraordinary feat in the face of adversity.

32

HAJI PIR PASS, POK,
28 SEPTEMBER 1965

Maj. Dyal and his platoon commanders, having covered the length and breadth of the pass, secured the strategic location from all sides by deploying sentries. With the area now fortified, the time had come to relay the information to the battalion commander.

The pre-determined code word 'Chamak Tara' resonated through the crisp mountain air, signalling the triumphant completion of their mission to capture the Haji Pir Pass.

The signal navigated the military hierarchy, starting from the battalion headquarters of 1 Para. Like a relay race, it passed through the chain of command, reaching the brigade, the division, the corps and the command levels. Each transmission was a crucial link, and ultimately, the signal reached the pinnacle of military authority—the Army headquarters in New Delhi. For the first time, the Indian government had gained control over the situation created by the enemy.

Meanwhile, at Haji Pir, the soldiers of 1 Para found themselves in a challenging predicament. Hunger and fatigue had set in, and their supplies, including shakkarparas, were depleted. The only means of receiving sustenance was through a helicopter, but the prospect of flying into enemy territory, coupled with unfavourable weather conditions, made this option dangerous.

Facing a dire need for sustenance, Maj. Dyal surveyed the surroundings. He spotted a few goats grazing on the slopes and made a quick decision—to use them as a source of food. The soldiers rounded up the goats, and in a couple of hours, the aroma of roasted meat permeated the air as they utilized dry wood found in one of the enemy's shelters.

However, the makeshift feast had its limitations—the soldiers lacked condiments, even salt. Undeterred, they pressed on and ate the half-cooked, unsalted meat. Officers and jawans alike partook in the unusual feast, a testament to their resourcefulness.

After the impromptu meal, the troops took turns to rest, recuperating from the challenges they had faced. The camaraderie forged in adversity and the innovative spirit displayed by Maj. Dyal and his jawans showcased the resilience and determination of the Indian Army in navigating the complexities of warfare.

* * *

Just before the sun dipped below the horizon, casting an orange glow on the rugged terrain of the Haji Pir Pass, alert eyes from one of the platoons on the western perimeter spotted a section-sized patrol advancing towards the pass.

The platoon relayed this information to Maj. Dyal, who, recognizing the threat, ordered his troops to be ready for engagement.

The Indian soldiers monitored the approaching section, tension in the air as they wondered about the enemy's intentions.

As the figures drew closer, the Indians began counting— only ten soldiers. The perplexing realization raised more questions. Was this a distraction or was something more sinister at play?

Maj. Dyal, sensing the need for caution, dispatched patrols in all directions, creating a vigilant ring around the pass. The Indians, armed and poised, waited with bated breath as the Pakistani soldiers continued their ascent.

Observing the approaching men, Maj. Dyal discerned an unusual nonchalance in their demeanour. Despite rifles slung from their shoulders, the Pakistani soldiers appeared to be walking casually. It became evident that they harboured no anticipation of resistance, unaware that the Haji Pir Pass had fallen into Indian hands.

As the Pakistanis came within the firing range of Indian small arms, a stern voice rang out—a challenge from an Indian JCO, '*Ruk* (stop).'

The Pakistani soldiers stopped as the JCO demanded identification. The taut, tense stand-off was suddenly broken when one of the Pakistanis made a fateful move towards his weapon.

In that split second, the JCO nodded to an Indian soldier who fired a single shot. The man crumpled to the ground and blood began to pool under his body.

The JCO reiterated, '*Maine bola ruk* (I said, stop).'

Intense moments passed as the Indians and Pakistanis locked eyes, each side sizing up the other.

A voice broke the silence, 'Sir, my name is Captain Maqbool Bhat.'

Intrigued, the JCO queried, 'Why are you here?'

The Pakistani captain responded, 'Sir, we are visiting Haji Pir to seek the blessings of Pir baba.'

The revelation, however, had a disconcerting follow-up, 'Blessings for what?'

'To attack and destroy the Indians.'

The JCO, after a pause, ordered the disarming of the Pakistani soldiers.

One by one, they laid their weapons on the ground. Further instructions ordered them to march forward slowly, allowing the Indian troops to retrieve their weapons.

Once this was executed, the Pakistani soldiers were directed to continue moving towards the Haji Pir Pass.

The JCO guided Capt. Maqbool Bhat to where the Indian officers sat.

Maj. Dyal, informed of the unfolding events on the radio, greeted the Pakistani officer with a nod of recognition, 'Captain Maqbool Bhat?'

Noticing that the Indian was senior to him, the unarmed Pakistani captain saluted him.

His curiosity piqued, Maj. Dyal inquired, 'So what's your special training?'

Capt. Bhat replied with pride, 'Sir, I am a trained commando. I was trained in the Ranger school in Georgia, USA.'

Maj. Dyal gestured to a soldier, 'Search his pockets.'

A jawan patted his pockets and pulled out a few folded papers.

Maj. Dyal opened the first paper. It was a typed page and addressed to the Army Chief of Pakistan. The heading read, 'Resignation from Pakistan Army.'

'What's this?'

Capt. Bhat replied, 'Sir, I want to resign from the Pakistan Army. This is my application.'

'Why?'

'Sir, my father is admitted in a hospital in Lahore. He is very unwell. Last week, I asked for leave for half a day and it was turned down. Why should I continue in the Army when I can't even see my father when he needs me the most?'

Maj. Dyal unfolded the remaining three sheets of papers. His eyes widened as he took in the detailed maps depicting 1 Para headquarters in Uri, along with the armoury and the officers' mess. His gaze bore into the captured Pakistani officer as he inquired, 'Out with the truth.'

The captured officer met Maj. Dyal's stare, his response cutting through the tense silence, 'Sir, my orders are to attack and eliminate all the officers of 1 Para in Uri.'

A heavy silence descended, the Indian soldiers tensing visibly, their determination palpable like coiled springs. Maj. Dyal's gaze swept across the surroundings before settling on Capt. Bhat.

When Maj. Dyal spoke again, his voice was measured but laced with resolve, 'And what fate do you think awaits you now?'

The captured officer's eyes fell to the ground, his plea filled with desperation, 'Please, sir, spare our lives. We will comply with any demand you make.'

The surroundings hung in a moment of charged anticipation, the weight of the decision looming heavy as Maj. Dyal contemplated his next action.

He called the adjutant, Capt. J.S. Bindra, and briefed him.

Thereafter, the Pakistanis were apprehended as Prisoners of War (POWs).

33

HAJI PIR PASS, POK, 29 AUGUST 1965

At 4 a.m., Maj. Arvinder Singh arrived with the remaining troops of Delta Company at the Haji Pir Pass after handing over Ledwali Gali to Maj. Patil and his Bravo Company.

As soon as he met Maj. Dyal, he greeted him, 'Good morning, sir.'

Maj. Dyal replied, 'Good morning, Major Arvinder Singh.'

'Sir, we need to send patrols deeper into the western side to see if the enemy is planning a counter-attack.'

'We have already secured all the heights surrounding the Haji Pir Pass, Major. We are safe here and I've been assured that 19 Punjab is likely to join us soon.'

'I still feel we should send a patrol deeper to check, particularly the ring contour on the west.'

'Okay. Let's do it in the night.'

Maj. Arvinder Singh thereafter chose Sub. Siri Chand, the platoon commander of 12 Platoon from Delta Company, for the recce. With a decisive tone, Maj. Arvinder instructed, 'Take your platoon after sunset, Siri Chand sahab. If you spot the enemy at the ring contour, dislodge them on your own. Otherwise, assess their strength and return.'

Sub. Siri Chand, displaying a crisp salute, affirmed his understanding, 'Ji, sahab.'

An hour after sunset, Sub. Siri Chand led his platoon towards the ring contour.

Maj. Arvinder Singh, relying on the strategic acumen of his platoon commanders, braced for the task that lay ahead, knowing that the outcome could influence the course of the operations in the Haji Pir region.

Sub. Siri Chand, a seasoned tactician in his late thirties, gathered his platoon upon their arrival in the designated area. The time was now 10 p.m.

In the dim light, he addressed his soldiers with a composed demeanour, '*Hamara* target *woh* contour line *hai. Humko pata nahin hai wahan dushman hai ya nahin. Agar wahan jyada dushman ke sainik honge, to hum* attack *nahin karenge. Yeh* suicide mission *nahin hai. Hum wapas aakar sabko lekar chalenge aur bada* attack *karenge. Koi bhi mere* order *se pehle* firing *nahin karega. Theek hai?* (Our target is that contour line. We don't know if enemy soldiers are there or not. If there are many enemy soldiers, then we will not attack. This is not a suicide mission. We will come back and take everyone along for a bigger attack. No one will fire unless I order. Is that clear?)'

The soldiers nodded their assent.

With the platoon on the move again, three sections advanced under the leadership of their respective section commanders, who were naiks and havildars. The stealthy progress was important to avoid detection in case the enemy had already reached. As they approached the contour line, Sub. Siri Chand, a silhouette against the dark sky, utilized his binoculars to assess the situation while the rest of the platoon sought cover behind tree trunks and rocks.

What Sub. Siri Chand witnessed through his binoculars startled him. Enemy forces had indeed gathered there in substantial numbers. In response, he instructed everyone to hold their positions and proceeded to the left, crawling on his stomach. Reaching the edge of a precipice, he peered into the valley below. The sight alarmed him further as he observed vehicles parked, a long line of porters and enemy soldiers heading towards the contour line. It became evident that his thirty-five soldiers could not take on such a sizeable force. Sub. Siri Chand signalled for everyone to retreat.

By the time Platoon 12 returned to the Haji Pir Pass, the clock had struck three in the morning. Sub. Siri Chand conveyed the news to Maj. Arvinder Singh, 'Sir, *dushman ki nafri saath ke lagbhag hai. Neeche* valley *se aur dushman upar aa raha hai* (Sir, there are around sixty enemy soldiers. From below in the valley, more enemy soldiers are on the way up).'

Maj. Arvinder Singh, maintaining his composure, responded, '*Theek hai*, Siri Chand sahab. 12 Platoon *ko aaram karne ke liye kaho* (Okay, Siri Chand sahab, 12 Platoon can rest for now).'

Sub. Siri Chand saluted and left, disappearing into the night.

Maj. Arvinder met Maj. Dyal and said, 'Sir, the patrol has spotted enemy troops at the ring contour.'

'How many?'

'Around sixty, but more are on the way. Once they strengthen, it will be difficult to push them back and we might lose Haji Pir. This is a do-or-die situation.'

Maj. Arvinder quickly shared all the details with Maj. Dyal.

The capture of Haji Pir hung in the balance as Maj. Dyal contemplated his next move in the face of an impending challenge.

After ordering Maj. Arvinder Singh to prepare to attack the enemy troops at the ring contour, he conveyed the situation to the battalion headquarters.

The battalion headquarters, now based in Ledwali Gali, sent this information to the brigade commander. Understanding the seriousness of the situation, as expected, Brig. Bakshi instructed the battalion to remove the enemy from the ring contour line and take control of this vital location. If the enemy wasn't removed promptly, they might regroup at the ring contour and launch a counter-attack, potentially reclaiming Haji Pir from 1 Para.

As the battalion commander was now on his way to the Haji Pir Pass, he assigned the task to Maj. Dyal.

34

RING CONTOUR, WEST OF HAJI PIR PASS, POK, 30 AUGUST 1965

Maj. Arvinder Singh and around seventy soldiers of Delta Company left the Haji Pir Pass at 4 a.m. They first decided to climb the right shoulder of the pass to approach the contour line along the ridge.

There was no rain now and it was dark. Dawn was a little over two hours away. The improved visibility would become a problem for the Indians as they were the ones who were exposing themselves by moving. The soldiers moved as quickly as possible, so as to cover the maximum distance before daylight.

Taking precautions, finally, they were able to get to within 100 yards of the contour line without being seen.

Maj. Arvinder Singh surveyed the area of operation. The topography posed an obstacle here. The ridge, while strategically significant, permitted only a platoon-sized force to cross it at any given time. This limitation hindered launching a comprehensive assault. Acknowledging the challenges of the terrain, the Indian forces planned to use surprise to overcome the natural obstacles of the ridge.

Moving with precision along with his troops, Maj. Arvinder Singh, understanding the importance of timing, took charge and aggressively attacked the enemy's positions along the contour line. The enemy fired, but the audacity of the Indian attack unnerved them. Within minutes, the Indians had captured the entire contour line.

But right behind the contour line, there was another contour line. That's where the enemy was visible now. Maj. Arvinder Singh knew that the only way to attack the second contour line was by exposing themselves in the gap between the two.

Meanwhile, the dynamics of the battle began to evolve. In the intervening period, while the Indian forces were contemplating their moves, the enemy ranks were swelling with reinforcements. The realization dawned on Maj. Arvinder Singh and his men that the foe was not only well-entrenched, but also outnumbered them.

Undeterred by the odds against them, Maj. Arvinder Singh pressed on, his determination unwavering even in the face of adversity. The clash between the two forces intensified as the Indian commander sought to gain a foothold on the second contour line, inching closer despite the odds.

In that fleeting moment, the enemy soldiers found themselves in a precarious position, immersed in the task of digging trenches when the daring attack unfolded. The echoes of the Indian advance reverberated through the air, disrupting their operations.

In a hurried response, the Pakistanis abandoned their digging implements, hastily casting them aside. The clang of shovels hitting the rocky ground was drowned out by the swift transition as the soldiers replaced their tools with the cold metal of their firearms. Taking positions, they braced themselves for the incoming assault, readying their weapons to counter the Indian advance.

The interplay of strategies, the ebb and flow of battle, unfolded in a relentless dance. The Indians aimed to penetrate the enemy's defences, but the opposition replied with a resilient defence, leveraging their numerical advantage. The landscape echoed with gunfire and the grit of soldiers engaged in a fierce struggle for dominance.

In the middle of the fight, Maj. Arvinder Singh and his troops showcased not just tactical skill but also unwavering bravery. These events changed the course of the battle, highlighting the determination of those fighting for control of the ridge.

With every new Indian attack, the enemy began to feel uneasy. They soon realized that the Indians weren't just launching assaults; they were methodically pushing into the core of enemy territory. The well-executed Indian manoeuvres forced the Pakistanis to regroup and strengthen their defences.

The ground was soon strewn with the fallen. The onslaught had taken its toll, and Indian soldiers, undeterred by the chaos, continued to press forward. Maj. Arvinder Singh, the courageous leader in the heart of the fray, heard the resonant war cry of the Ahirs, '*Dada Kishan ki jai*', a rallying call that echoed through the cacophony of battle, spurring the soldiers onward.

A fierce and close combat erupted as soldiers grappled with the Pakistanis at different spots. The battle's intensity showed no sign of letting up, and there was no break in the action.

Meanwhile, at the Haji Pir Pass, Maj. Dyal heard the sound of bombs and guns and started to move towards the ring contour. As he arrived at a position behind Maj. Arvinder Singh, he saw the soldiers of Delta Company were now fighting hand-to-hand with the enemy. That's when he saw Maj. Arvinder Singh bayonet and kill two enemy soldiers.

Maj. Dyal began to fire and move ahead. He spotted two enemy soldiers appear from behind the ridge and take aim at the fighting Indian jawans, and he got them in quick, successive shots.

In the middle of this intense exchange, the fog of battle descended upon Maj. Dyal. The chaotic symphony of gunfire and the cries of soldiers painted the landscape with an atmosphere of impending danger. As Maj. Dyal moved ahead, he had no clue he was about to be shot.

Suddenly, a burst of bullets found their mark, hitting Maj. Dyal squarely in the stomach. The impact was forceful, throwing him backward on to the rocky terrain. Instinctively, he glanced down, expecting to feel searing pain, only to discover a surreal reprieve.

A stroke of fortune had intervened; the bullets had found an unexpected barrier. His gun and the sturdy webbing he wore had absorbed the impact, shielding him from the deadly bullets. The realization that none of the bullets had penetrated his body was met with a mix of relief and awe. In the middle of the firefight, Maj. Dyal found himself not incapacitated but resolute, ready to lead his men with determination despite the brush with a death-defying fate (a photograph of Maj. Dyal's gun with bullet marks is included in the image section).

In the commotion of battle, the spirit of Maj. Arvinder Singh faced an abrupt interruption too. A sharp impact struck him, forcing him to the ground. Despite the unbearable pain coursing through his body, Maj. Arvinder Singh summoned every ounce of strength, attempting to rise to his feet. However, his efforts were thwarted as searing agony emanated from his leg, rendering him incapacitated.

As Maj. Arvinder Singh grappled with the excruciating pain, a realization dawned upon him—he was not alone in this struggle. When he took in the scene all around him, the chaos of battle unveiled a fallen jawan from his own company. Their eyes locked in a moment of shared understanding, and Maj. Arvinder Singh recognized the fallen soldier. It was Naik (Nk) Hira Singh.

Determined to extend a helping hand, Maj. Arvinder Singh said, 'I need to help you, Hira Singh.'

In response, Nk Hira Singh, displaying a blend of patriotism and bravery, reassured his officer, '*Sahab, meri chinta mat karao, aap aage chalo. Hamein dushman ko harana hai. Meri* LMG *le lo* (Sir, don't worry about me. You move forward. We have to defeat the enemy. Take my LMG).'

Despite the debilitating pain in his leg, Maj. Arvinder Singh mustered the strength to stand, leaning on his weapon for support. Limping forward with difficulty, he pressed on, each step weighed down by both physical agony and the emotional burden of losing the jawans of his company. The urgency of the battlefield necessitated that he forge ahead, determined to fulfil the mission.

A few fleeting seconds later, Maj. Arvinder Singh, compelled by an innate sense of responsibility, turned to look back at Nk Hira Singh. The reality unfolded before him; Hira Singh had succumbed to his wounds. In that poignant moment, Maj. Arvinder Singh, amid the chaos of battle, grappled with the profound weight of loss, the sacrifice of a jawan etched indelibly into the narrative of valour and camaraderie on the battlefield.

The Indian forces, fuelled by determination, persistently fought the enemy, steadily moving closer to victory with every passing moment.

In the heat of the battle, L/Hav. Umrao Singh exhibited remarkable courage and determination. Recognizing the threat posed by the enemy's MMG, which could cause substantial damage, he took it upon himself to neutralize the threat. Undeterred by the hail of bullets, L/Hav. Umrao Singh fearlessly charged towards the MMG, covering the open distance in mere seconds.

As bullets whizzed past him, he closed in on the enemy position and hurled a grenade that silenced the MMG operators. Tragically, not without sacrifice, as Umrao Singh sustained injuries from the enemy's final barrage of bullets. Despite the ultimate sacrifice he made, his brave and decisive actions played a pivotal role in turning the tide of the combat in favour of India.

After a gruelling hour of conflict, a shift occurred on the battlefield. The enemy, overwhelmed by the determination of the Indian forces, began to lose their nerve. The momentum shifted decisively and the inevitability of retreat began to loom large over the opposing forces. The Indians, aware of the signs that their adversaries were faltering, sensed the shift in the battle.

The Pakistani officers, their voices punctuating the chaos, called their troops back. Speaking in Punjabi, they conveyed a message of vulnerability. By this juncture, only nine Indians remained alongside Maj. Arvinder Singh.

The Pakistani soldiers, their officers leading the way, turned and retreated from the contested ground. The echoes of the battlefield slowly subsided as the enemy forces, disheartened and overpowered, yielded to the indomitable spirit of Delta Company of 1 Para.

By 10.30 a.m., the dust settled on the battleground, marking a triumph. Delta Company, under the leadership of Maj. Arvinder Singh, stood victorious. The coveted ring contour, a symbol of strategic significance, had been conquered. The resilience, sacrifice and valour displayed by the Indian forces in those pivotal moments etched a chapter of courage and determination into the annals of military history.

As the poignant aftermath unfolded, a sombre procession commenced on the terrain. The fallen heroes, both martyred and injured soldiers, including the valiant but badly injured Maj. Arvinder Singh, were carefully placed on stretchers. The weight of sacrifice and the echoes of the struggle hung heavy in the air as they began their solemn journey back to the Haji Pir Pass.

In addition to the captured Pathans, around 150 local Kashmiri youths were employed to carry the martyred and injured officers and jawans all the way from the Haji Pir Pass to Uri.

In recognition of his extraordinary bravery and initiative, L/Hav. Umrao Singh was posthumously awarded the Vir Chakra, a testament to his indomitable spirit and selfless dedication to the nation.

Meanwhile, Maj. Dyal, embodying the steadfast spirit of a seasoned commander, chose to return to the hard-won ring contour. With a resolute gaze fixed on the landscape, he issued orders to the remaining troops, directing them to consolidate the position. The battle-hardened soldiers, their fatigue momentarily set aside, rallied under Maj. Dyal's command to fortify the just-conquered territory.

35

RING CONTOUR, WEST OF HAJI PIR
PASS, POK, 30 AUGUST 1965

The ring contour, a site of fierce struggle and triumph, became a symbol of the indomitable spirit of Delta Company. As the wounded were carried away, Maj. Dyal stood among the rocky outcrops, overseeing the consolidation efforts, his determination ensuring that the gains achieved in battle would be secured.

The landscape bore witness to the juxtaposition of victory and loss, of soldiers moving with determination to tend to their fallen brothers and a commander standing resolute in the face of the aftermath. The echoes of conflict lingered in the air, a reminder of the sacrifices made on that hallowed ground. The tale of Haji Pir, etched in the annals of military history, spoke of courage, camaraderie and the enduring spirit of those who faced the war.

Maj. Dyal had observed the enemy forces climbing the slope towards the contour line just a while ago.

He addressed the troops, '*Dushman iss* contour line *ko* recapture *karne ke liye phir se* attack *karega. Hum ko taiyyar rehna hai* (The enemy will try to retake this contour line by attacking again. We must be ready).'

His eyes then began to search for the intelligence NCO of Delta Company, Nk Jai Singh, and found him sitting a few feet away.

Maj. Dyal walked up to him and saw that he was bleeding heavily from his leg due to a bullet injury.

Maj. Dyal asked, '*Aap theek ho* (Are you all right)?'

Nk Jai Singh looked up and replied, '*Ji sahab, main theek hoon, sahab.*'

'*Aisa lagta toh nahin hai. Kya aap* FOO *ban sakte ho, aur* Captain Naidu *ke aane tak* direction *de sakte ho* (You don't seem okay. Can you operate as the FOO and give directions till Captain Naidu arrives)?'

'*Ji, sahab.*'

Maj. Dyal knew he could depend on Nk Jai Singh and asked another jawan to help him stop the bleeding.

After this, Maj. Dyal inspected the location minutely and called the CO to report, 'Sir, ring contour is secure now.'

'Well done, Major Dyal. What's the situation now?'

'Sir, we have had a few casualties. I'll signal the numbers later. Major Arvinder Singh has been hit in the leg too and has been evacuated along with other injured and martyred soldiers.'

'Okay. Has the enemy been pushed back sufficiently, or are you expecting a counter-attack? Do you need more troops?'

'Sir, I can see them climbing along the slopes. I need the artillery support now. The intelligence JCO of Delta Company will act as FOO from here.'

'Roger. I'm sending Captain Naidu right away. Major Dyal?'

'Yes, sir?'

'The attack was too impulsive. Had we waited for more troops, we could have won the feature without so many casualties.'

'No, sir. Surprise was necessary. I can see a large number of pits being dug here. From the dimensions, it is clear that these were not just trenches and bunkers, but also mortar positions. My appreciation is that the location was being readied for positioning a battalion headquarters of the Pakistan Army.'

'And therefore, had Major Arvinder Singh and the Delta boys waited for more troops to join, they would have built up in strength there?'

'Yes, sir.'

'You are in the front, Major Dyal, so I agree with your appreciation. Any captured arms and ammunition?'

'Nine LMGs, three 3-inch mortars, radios, maps, etc.'

'Which enemy battalion was this?'

'20 Punjab of the Pakistan Army, sir.'

'Great work done by you, Major Arvinder and Delta Company.'

'Thank you, sir.'

During the day, the Pakistan Army counter-attacked twice, trying to sneak in from different directions, but were beaten back both times.

Finally, at around 4 p.m., they stopped terrain attacks and instead started bombing the Indians by using their artillery from the deep (far away). The bombs kept falling till last light, but by then, the Indians had secured themselves well and sustained little damage.

36

HAJI PIR PASS, POK, 31 AUGUST 1965

Early in the morning, the Indian troops were overjoyed when they spotted an Indian Air Force MI-4 helicopter approach them and hover over Haji Pir. The helicopter dropped food, ammunition and medical supplies. The Indians had been eating shakkarparas since 25 August and had had only some half-cooked goat meat since their arrival at the Haji Pir Pass.

The Indian officers and jawans ate gratefully.

As soon as they had finished eating, the commander of Charlie Company, Maj. J.C.M. Rao, received a call on the radio from the CO. Charlie Company had arrived at Haji Pir in the morning.

'Good morning, sir.'

'Major Rao, I want you to leave with your company from Haji Pir right away and help us consolidate the contour line here. How soon can you leave?'

'We are ready, sir. We can leave in thirty minutes at the most.'

Maj. Rao placed the radio set down and quickly assembled his company. Within minutes he was addressing his troops, '*Mere bahadur jawanon, hum ko ek bahut hi badi zimmedaari di gayi hai. Humko abhi* ring contour *ke liye nikalna hai. Kal, hamari* Delta Company *ke bahadur jawanon ne jeet haasil ki thi. Lekin dushman ki nafri jyada hai. Ab Bharat Mata ki raksha ke liye hamein jana hai* (My brave soldiers, we have been given a big responsibility. We must leave for the ring contour right away. Yesterday, the brave soldiers of Delta Company had achieved success there. But the enemy is assembling in large numbers. Now we must go to protect Mother India).'

In under thirty minutes, the JCOs and jawans of Charlie Company left Haji Pir for the ring contour feature. They reached their destination at 10 a.m. When they arrived, there was a pause in the enemy's attack.

Maj. Rao met Maj. Dyal.

'Charlie Company reporting, sir.'

'Major Rao, let me brief you about the situation here. 20 Punjab of the Pakistan Army is on the other side. This is a pure Pakistan Army battalion, not the mixed ones we were dealing with earlier. Yesterday, they had counter-attacked us twice. This morning, they have already attacked us once. We have beaten them, but they have succeeded in creating a launch pad on the south-west side, somewhere between our positions and theirs. This position needs to be taken. Only then will we have consolidated this ring contour.'

'Yes, sir.'

Maj. Dyal had made a rough map on the ground with a stick.

'I want you to take your company and knock them out.'

'Yes, sir.'

Maj. Rao left after saluting Maj. Dyal. He knew he could depend on his men, but he also knew this would be a difficult mission.

Following an hour of meticulous briefing and preparations, Maj. Rao, demonstrating tactical acumen and valour, spearheaded an assault on the commanding feature. His allied forces, comprising the resolute jawans of Charlie Company, stood ready for the engagement.

As the assault unfolded, the air resonated with the battle cries of the Jat warriors. The spirited jawans, invoking their heritage and strength, shouted, '*Jat balwan, jai bhagwan*' (the Jat is powerful, victory be to god). The echoes of their collective cries reverberated across the rugged terrain, a proclamation of their resolve and commitment to the mission.

A short yet intense encounter ensued. The brave jawans of Charlie Company, fuelled by their training, camaraderie and the indomitable spirit of their war cry, engaged with a section-sized force of 20 Punjab from Pakistan. The feature, a critical vantage point in the theatre of war, became the focal point of the clash between two determined forces.

After a fierce struggle, the jawans of Charlie Company emerged victorious, successfully neutralizing the enemy force that had held the feature. The triumph, however, did not come without a cost. The Indian forces, in the middle of their valorous efforts, mourned the loss of two gallant jawans who made the ultimate sacrifice. Additionally, eight others displayed resilience in the face of adversity, sustaining injuries in the line of duty.

As soon as Maj. Dyal received the information, he realized that the Indians had once again consolidated the ring contour feature.

He called up his CO: 'Sir, the ring contour continues to be with us.'

'Good. I want you to move to the base of the Bisali feature now and stay put there as a reserve. 4 Rajput Battalion is on their way to capture it from the enemy.'

'Yes, sir.'

The Pakistan Army apparently offered a prize of Rs 50,000 for the head of Maj. Ranjit Singh Dyal. This was discovered through the radio intercept of a Pakistani officer telling his comrade, 'I wish I had Major Dyal's head. I could get fifty thousand rupees from the Pakistani Army.'

—*P.C. Katoch, 'Battle of Haji Pir: The Army's Glory in 1965'*, Journal of Defence Studies, *Vol. 9, No. 3, July–September 2015, p. 70.*

37

BISALI FEATURE, POK,
1 SEPTEMBER 1965

Following a night-long trek through challenging terrain, the soldiers of 1 Para reached the FUP at the Bisali feature.

Bisali, standing at an altitude of 11,200 feet, was essentially a mountain along the Uri–Poonch axis. It was on the west side of the axis, with Bedori its formidable counterpart on the east, which 19 Punjab had conquered in its second attempt on 29 August 1965.

The journey had tested their endurance, but their spirits remained unbroken. Upon arrival, the warriors took up defensive positions, their tired bodies and hungry stomachs a testament to the physical toll exacted by the trek.

For the next three days, they patiently held their ground, awaiting further orders in anticipation of the unfolding strategic landscape.

Meanwhile, on a parallel front, the 4 Rajput Battalion, having made steady progress from the left (east) since D-Day, received orders to launch an assault on the Bisali feature. The stage was set for a fierce confrontation as the Rajputs prepared for the battle.

As the night of 4 September 1965 descended, the Rajputs engaged in a struggle to capture the Bisali feature. The clash was intense, marked by the thunderous echoes of gunfire and the courage of soldiers in the thick of battle.

In a testament to their fortitude, the Rajputs managed to seize control of the strategic feature, their victory echoing through the night.

However, the ebbs and flows of war proved unpredictable as the Indians were to realize three hours later. The enemy, undeterred by the initial setback, swiftly reorganized their forces and launched a counter-attack with determined ferocity.

In the ensuing chaos, they managed to retake the coveted Bisali feature, reversing the gains made by the Rajputs. The battleground bore witness to the grim reality of warfare, with a significant number of Indian soldiers sacrificing their lives in a valiant attempt to protect and retain control of the feature.

1 Para was not deployed as retrieving Bisali from the enemy was not considered an operational possibility or need. The brigade headquarters evaluated the situation and determined that committing 1 Para Battalion to this operation would not yield a strategic advantage proportional to the potential cost in lives and resources. Consequently, the battalion remained on standby, prepared to support other critical operations as needed.

The night, which had initially witnessed the triumph of capturing the Bisali feature, transformed into a haunting reminder of the relentless nature of conflict. The sacrifice of the martyred Indians, who had valiantly defended the strategic position, resonated across the battlefield. It was time for an organized retreat by the Indians.

After Bisali fell, 1 Para was ordered to return to the Haji Pir Pass on 5 September 1965.

38

HAJI PIR PASS, POK,
7 SEPTEMBER 1965

Maj. Dyal and his troops had been stationed at the Haji Pir Pass for over a week, and the next phase of their mission was set to begin. The commanding officer contacted him on the radio, saying, 'Major Dyal, it's time for us to take action again. I trust the boys are well-rested and prepared.'

'Yes, sir. We're ready.'

'93 Brigade forces are advancing northwards towards you. We need to secure the western area off the road to Kahuta bridge so that 19 Punjab and battalions of 93 Brigade can reach us. This will ensure we successfully cut off the entire Haji Pir bulge from Pakistan once and for all.'

Maj. Dyal enthusiastically responded, 'Yes, sir.'

'All right, your next mission is to capture Point 8786 near Khoranakka, just north of the Gitian feature at Point

8777. Intelligence reports suggest it's held by a platoon of 20 Punjab Battalion of Pakistan.'

'Yes, sir.'

On the fateful night of 7 September 1965, the clock striking 10.30 marked the commencement of a critical mission led by Maj. Dyal. Alongside him were Maj. Rao and Maj. Patil, accompanied by the Bravo and Charlie Companies. Their mission: to advance towards the first objective, Point 8786. The meticulous planning had foreseen the cloak of darkness as their ally, and the troops were prepared for a night attack.

As the soldiers set forth into the inky blackness, it started to rain.

By the stroke of midnight, the covert manoeuvre had successfully carried them to the final 75 yards, all achieved without betraying their presence to the enemy. The rain had helped, too. However, the terrain presented an unexpected obstacle—a daunting cliff 50 feet high obstructed their path. At the summit, the adversary lay in wait, unaware of the approaching Indian Army.

The moment of contemplation was shattered when the enemy detected the presence of the Indians. A fusillade erupted as two MMGs opened fire from either side of the cliff, accompanied by the staccato rhythm of an LMG positioned in the middle. The element of surprise had been lost, and a fierce engagement ensued.

In the face of this situation, Maj. Dyal assessed the need for decisive action. In a moment of command, he directed Capt. Naidu to position himself at the cliff's edge and guide accurate artillery bombardment on to the enemy positions. The orders were executed promptly, with the hope of neutralizing the threat.

Regrettably, the proximity of the Indian forces to the enemy positions resulted in a tragic turn of events. As the artillery shells rained down, a few rounds inadvertently struck the Indian troops, causing casualties. The urgency of the situation necessitated an immediate halt to the artillery bombardment.

In the middle of the chaotic engagement, Maj. Rao, displaying remarkable leadership and audacity, made a decision to lead his jawans of Charlie Company up the formidable cliff. The ascent, fraught with challenges, unfolded as a test of both skill and resilience. Maj. Dyal, recognizing the gravity of the situation, provided covering fire to shield the advancing troops.

The climb, though arduous, initially proved successful. However, as the first jawan of Charlie Company, Nk Amar Singh, section commander of 7 Platoon, reached the precipice and raised his head to launch a grenade at the entrenched enemy, tragedy struck. A swift, lethal shot found its mark, and Nk Amar Singh fell, his sacrifice marking the price paid for every inch gained.

Undeterred by the loss, Maj. Rao, alongside a small group of Indian jawans, persevered and reached the pinnacle of the cliff. In the impenetrable darkness, their visibility severely limited, Maj. Rao forged ahead, attempting to lead his troops in a cohesive attack. However, in the darkness and chaos, tragedy befell as he too was struck by enemy fire.

In the unfolding drama, Maj. Patil emerged as a beacon of determination. Scaling the cliff from the left side, he navigated the terrain with skill. A marksmanship feat by Lance Naik (L/Nk) Krishan Lal, one of his LMG operators, neutralized one of the MMGs, albeit at the cost of L/Nk Krishan Lal being wounded in the process.

Despite reaching the top of the cliff, the Indian forces found themselves unable to dislodge the entrenched enemy. The disadvantage of the darkness, combined with the tenacity of the opposition, proved to be formidable obstacles. The gallantry displayed by Maj. Rao, the fallen Nk Amar Singh and the wounded warriors underscored the harsh realities of war, where every inch gained came at the highest cost. As the night continued to unfold, the fate of the cliffside battle remained uncertain.

With the fight still raging, the CO called Maj. Dyal on the radio, 'I'm sending Delta Company now.'

'Okay, sir.'

That night, another calamity befell the Indian forces, adding a layer of complexity to the situation. The enemy, demonstrating cunningness, infiltrated the communication network of the Indian troops. In a sinister turn of events, they began providing false positions for the incoming artillery bombs, effectively turning a potent weapon against its own wielders.

The chaos and confusion sown by this misdirection led to a tragic repetition of the earlier aerial bombardment, claiming more lives and inflicting additional injuries among the Indians.

The turn of events cast a shadow over the battlefield, further complicating the efforts of the Indian officers to regain control. Before counter-measures could be implemented, the rain of bombs descended once again, wreaking havoc and amplifying the toll on the Indian forces.

The fight for Point 8786 had evolved into a daunting struggle, with the Indian forces grappling not only against a determined adversary but also against the effects of internal miscommunication.

The pivotal entry of Delta Company into the fray, occurring two hours later, injected fresh determination into the Indian forces. However, the toll of the battle was undeniable. Dozens of Indian soldiers had been wounded, some gravely, and many had made the ultimate sacrifice.

The enemy, against the odds, continued to hold Point 8786, turning the location into a bastion of resistance. The battlefield, now shrouded in the darkness of uncertainty and loss, echoed with the resilience of those who fought against formidable odds.

In the absence of Maj. Arvinder Singh, who had been evacuated to a hospital due to a severe leg injury sustained during the battle at the ring contour, the leadership mantle of Delta Company now rested on the shoulders of Capt. Gurung.

This marked Capt. Gurung's inaugural foray into active combat, a stark contrast to his previous experiences in sportsmanship and marksmanship. Undeterred by the challenging circumstances, Capt. Gurung rallied his troops, and together, they assembled at the base of Point 8786, ready to face the trials of the battlefield.

Tragedy struck as a shell found its mark, hitting Capt. Gurung and sending him to the ground, his promising leadership and resilience extinguished in an instant. This poignant moment marked the first casualty among the officers of 1 Para, casting a sombre shadow over the hearts of all who witnessed the sacrifice.

The fight continued throughout the night and well into the next day. The formidable Indian forces, despite facing adversity and the loss of their gallant leader, pressed on with determination. The battlefield echoed with the cacophony of gunfire, the cries of soldiers and the thuds of explosions as the struggle for Point 8786 continued to unfold.

As the sun dipped low on the horizon, the toll on the Indian forces became apparent. One officer and ten jawans had been martyred, and a staggering seventy-two soldiers, JCOs and officers were left injured, each bearing the physical and emotional scars of the battle. However, the indomitable spirit of the Indian forces prevailed, and at the cost of significant sacrifice, they emerged victorious, capturing Point 8786.

At 6 p.m., the clock signalled a bittersweet moment of triumph and reflection after the hard-fought victory.

* * *

Brig. Zorawar Chand Bakshi was awarded the prestigious Maha Vir Chakra for planning and executing the successful capture of the Haji Pir Pass.

Maj. Ranjit Singh Dyal was awarded the Maha Vir Chakra for his exceptional leadership and valour. L/Hav. Umrao Singh, a brave member of Delta Company, was posthumously awarded the Vir Chakra, while Capt. M.D. Naidu was honoured with the Vir Chakra too. Additionally, Capt. M.M.P.S. Dhillon of Bravo Company was bestowed with the Sena Medal, and Sub. Arjun Singh of Delta Company was posthumously conferred the Sena Medal.

Further, 1 Para Battalion was awarded 'Battle Honour Haji Pir' and 'Theatre Honour Jammu and Kashmir (1965)'.

The remarkable success of 1 Para in capturing the Haji Pir Pass can be attributed to two factors: the display of bold leadership qualities exhibited by the commanders at every echelon of the unit's hierarchy, and the physical fitness levels maintained by all ranks of Sikhs, Dogras, Jats and Ahirs within the formation. The combination of strong leadership, characterized by strategic acumen, tactical prowess and the ability to inspire and guide troops effectively played a crucial role in orchestrating and executing the mission.

Moreover, the commitment to training among all members of 1 Para contributed significantly to the success. The soldiers' robust physical training not only enhanced their individual performance but also bolstered the unit's overall combat capabilities. This commitment to training fostered endurance, agility and resilience, ensuring that the troops were well-prepared for the demanding and challenging terrain they encountered during the mission to capture the Haji Pir Pass.

But there was one final Pakistani resistance in a hill feature called Gitian that was yet to be snuffed out and this task was given by Brig. Zorawar Chand Bakshi to the just arrived 6 Dogra Battalion.

After capturing the Haji Pir Pass, a senior JCO from 1 Para gathered 150 local Bakarwal residents to assist in hauling stretchers carrying the injured. Following the commanding officer's directive, they were promised double the standard rates for civil porters, amounting to over Rs 4 per porter—a substantial sum at the time. These porters, hailing from economically disadvantaged border areas, surprised everyone in 1 Para when they declined to accept the payment, saying that their efforts were a heartfelt contribution to Mother India.

—*Colonel Awadhesh Kumar, Special Forces (paraphrased)*

39

GITIAN FEATURE, KAHUTA, POK, 15–23 SEPTEMBER 1965

As soon as 6 Dogra Battalion arrived at the Haji Pir Pass, it was tasked with attacking the Gitian feature from the east (Kahuta side). The attack was scheduled for 15 September 1965.

The battalion, under the command of Lt Col S.S. Khokhar, departed for Kahuta under the veil of twilight. On their way, they encountered and seized control of a small feature known as Dogra Hill, which was fiercely guarded by a section of the Pakistan Army. Leaving Delta Company behind to secure the captured position, the rest of 6 Dogra Battalion pressed onward towards Kahuta.

Equipped with their standard-issue weapons, the battalion also carried six MMGs and two 3-inch mortars, along with approximately 250 bombs, to support their advance.

However, as dusk turned into night, it began to drizzle and the temperature plunged below 10 degrees Celsius.

The rain soaked through their clothing, burdening them with added weight, prompting many soldiers to discard their blankets and steel helmets to alleviate the discomfort. However, they pulled their balaclava caps tightly over their heads, chins and necks. Despite the weather, their spirits remained unbroken as they moved forward.

When the soldiers reached Kahuta at sunrise, they occupied the local school and the surrounding slopes. With nightfall approaching, they sought refuge in the veranda and classrooms of the school to rest.

Maj. Hazara Singh, the seasoned quartermaster of 6 Dogra, spoke to the commanding officer: 'Sir, since the hills surround us and the peaks haven't been secured, we shouldn't use the school's veranda to rest.'

Respecting Maj. Hazara's experience, the decision was made to avoid the school at night.

Around midnight, enemy fire erupted from the hills towards the school, but Maj. Hazara's caution helped save many lives.

The Dogras returned fire, engaging in a fierce battle that raged throughout the night. Remarkably, there were no casualties on the Indian side. As dawn broke, calm descended upon the area once more.

As per the intelligence they had received, the Gitian feature was under the control of two companies of the Pakistan Army. Meanwhile, on 17 September 1965, 19 Punjab, also stationed at Kahuta, received orders to secure the slopes, establishing a foothold for the forthcoming attack by 6 Dogra.

The enemy fired at the Indian positions for the whole day and 19 Punjab fired back at them. Since the prospect of assaulting this position seemed daunting, a decision was made to opt for an unexpected approach—attacking from a cliff, catching the enemy off guard.

Lt Col S.S. Khokhar, the commanding officer, 6 Dogra, gave the orders to attack at 2.30 a.m. on 19 September 1965. However, the brigade postponed the attack, first to 20 September and then to 21 September.

The Gitian hill consisted of three smaller features at its top. These were named Tree Hill, Hut Hill and Knoll. It was decided that Bravo Company, commanded by Maj. Darshan Singh Lalli, would capture Tree Hill, and Charlie Company, commanded by Maj. J.P. Makkar, would capture Hut Hill. Alpha Company was held in reserve. Knoll was to be captured later, when the other two features had been secured.

After the commanding officer had finished his briefing, he looked at Maj. Darshan Singh Lalli and said, 'This is not going to be easy, Major Lalli.'

He replied, 'Sir, my troops and I are ready.'

Maj. Makkar echoed the same sentiment.

After saluting the CO, Maj. Darshan Singh Lalli said, 'Sir, I'll meet you tomorrow morning at Tree Hill, dead or alive. That's my promise.'

The CO said, 'All the best.'

Under the cover of darkness, both companies commenced their advance after sunset. As they approached to within 200 yards of their target, the enemy unleashed a barrage of gunfire. Undeterred, the Dogras retaliated, their battle cry of *Jwala Mata ki jai* echoing through the air as they charged into the storm of bullets.

At the forefront of this fearless charge stood L/Hav. Naubat Ram, exhibiting unparalleled bravery. With unwavering resolve, he hurled grenades at the enemy positions, successfully neutralizing one of their LMG posts. Despite sustaining three bullet wounds during the exchange, he refused to be evacuated, determined to continue leading his troops forward.

Soon, the soldiers were fighting hand to hand. The Indians were lobbing grenades into the bunkers and trenches of the enemy. The fight lasted all night and by first light, Bravo Company had captured Tree Hill and Charlie Company had captured Hut Hill. L/Hav. Naubat Ram was, however, tragically killed by the burst from the enemy's weapons just as they were retreating.

Maj. Darshan Singh Lalli was martyred during the action as well. He lived up to the promise he had made to the commanding officer of 6 Dogra Battalion.

The responsibility of leading Bravo Company then fell to Capt. Zoru Chaudhary (not to be confused with Brig. Zoru Bakshi, or Brig. Zora Singh). Just after sunrise, the Pakistanis launched a fierce counter-attack in a desperate attempt to retake Tree Hill.

Capt. Zoru Chaudhary called the mortar officer, Second Lieutenant (2 Lt) Surjit Singh Sandhu, for support. Thereafter, the subaltern rose to the occasion and in a coordinated defence, repulsed the enemy attack. A few hours later, the enemy attacked Tree Hill again and yet again, but was repulsed.

Meanwhile, Charlie Company was counter-attacked too. Maj. J.P. Makkar was injured in this skirmish and had to be evacuated. That's when two platoons of 19 Punjab, under the leadership of Maj. Ranvir Singh, were sent to Hut Hill. With reinforced forces, Charlie Company fought well, but Maj. Ranvir Singh was martyred while leading from the front.

At Tree Hill, Alpha Company was also ordered to further bolster Indian defences. Soon after they arrived, Alpha Company suffered heavy casualties. 2 Lt Sandhu, mortar officer, was also sent forward to Tree Hill. The enemy counter-attacked twice again during the day but failed to remove the Indians occupying Tree Hill.

A small feature called Point 7604, located between Tree Hill and Hut Hill, was still held by the enemy. 2 Lt Sandhu was tasked with clearing it and he led an attack with one JCO and twenty sepoys. As soon as the Dogras attacked, shouting, '*Jwala Mata ki jai*', the enemy just ran away.

After this, the enemy retreated deep westwards and the Gitian feature came completely under Indian control. But it came at a heavy cost. Three officers (Maj. Darshan Singh Lalli, Maj. Ranvir Singh of 19 Punjab and Capt. Parthasarthy) and twenty-one soldiers had laid down their lives. In addition, six officers, four JCOs and sixty-six soldiers were wounded.

The Pakistanis left behind their thirty dead and retrieved around 100 wounded.

L/Hav. Naubat Ram was awarded the Maha Vir Chakra (posthumous). Maj. Darshan Singh Lalli, Maj. Ranvir Singh and Hav. Kaushi Ram were awarded Vir Chakras (all posthumous). The Sena Medal was awarded to Maj. H.S. Sachdev, Sub. Hans Raj and Sep. Jarnail Singh (posthumous). In addition, those who were Mentioned-in-Dispatches included Maj. B.K. Mehta, Maj. K.B. Thapa and Sep. Ronki Ram. And finally, the brave 6 Dogra Battalion was awarded the Battle Honour, Gitian (Haji Pir).

PART 4

CODE NAME: OPERATION FAULAD

Capture of Raja Hill and link-up
with 1 Para—attack from
Poonch (south side)

40

93 BRIGADE HEADQUARTERS, POONCH, 2 SEPTEMBER 1965

Let us rewind the story to understand the attack by the Indian forces from the south side of the bulge (Poonch side).

At the 93 Brigade headquarters located in Poonch, Brig. Zora Singh was conducting the O group operational briefing. All the commanding officers of the battalions under the command of 93 Brigade were present and stood before the sand model that replicated the features of the entire Poonch area.

These officers were heading 2 Sikh, 3 Dogra, 7 Madras, 3 Rajputana Rifles, 7 Sikh, 14 Kumaon, 3/11 Gorkha Rifles and 4/8 Gorkha Rifles Battalions. Out of these, the 2 Sikh Battalion had arrived in Poonch just a day before.

Brig. Zora Singh looked at Lt Col N.N. Khanna, commanding officer of 2 Sikh Battalion, and asked, 'How was your reconnaissance yesterday?'

Lt Col Khanna replied, 'Sir, we observed the enemy at the Raja feature from our Post 405 along the CFL. I had taken my platoon commanders and even section commanders for a closer look.'

'Good! What's your assessment, Colonel Khanna?'

'The enemy position looks formidable, sir. Do we have any maps of the area across the border to understand the topography better?'

The brigade commander shook his head and said, 'No, unfortunately not. But 3 Dogra has conducted several silent reconnaissance missions of the approach to Raja.' He turned to another officer and continued, 'Colonel Nair, go ahead and share your views.'

Lt Col R.B. Nair, commanding officer, 3 Dogra Battalion, started to speak, 'Sir, the approach to Raja is tricky. We will have to make use of our artillery powerfully before sending the infantry in.'

Brig. Zora Singh said, 'Okay, I want all eyes on the sand model here now. In the first phase of Operation Faulad, I want 3 Dogra to go in and capture Raja post. Colonel Nair, you are well-versed with the area, so you decide your strategy and give the orders. Once we succeed in capturing Raja, I want 2 Sikh Battalion to move forward along the ridge, cross the Raja post and capture Rani. Beyond it,' he leaned forward as he extended the wooden pointer and continued, 'as you can see here, is a small feature called Sur Tekri. According to our intelligence, this location is lightly held, so capture that as well. Colonel Khanna, you can issue your orders as you deem fit.'

Everyone kept quiet after Lt Col Nair and Lt Col Khanna had said 'Yes'.

But the brigade commander's eyes were still on the sand model. He continued after a few moments, 'After capturing Raja and Rani posts, we will begin phase two and continue to move northwards towards Kahuta. Maj. Megh Singh's force will clear the enemy-held features on the eastern side of our movement axis, and will also keep the enemy engaged by continuous firing from that side.'

One of the commanding officers asked, 'Sir, what is the condition of the road that connects the area north of Rani to Kahuta and further towards the Haji Pir Pass?'

Brig. Zora Singh replied, 'Well, the old road that was used for trade during the Mughal period is in a bad state due to disuse, but many stretches are still motorable, according to the information available with the brigade's intelligence.'

With the meeting over, Brig. Zora Singh issued his ORBAT. According to this, 3 Dogra Battalion was to attack and capture Raja feature on the night of 2 September 1965 and once that was achieved by midnight, 2 Sikh Battalion was to cross Raja, attack and capture Rani (also called Point 7702) before noon, followed by Sur Tekri farther north on the same day.

The 3 Dogra Battalion had been chosen for this attack from the Poonch side because it was well-versed with the area, and 2 Sikh was chosen because it was the strongest battalion with the maximum number of sportsmen and athletes in it.

The commanding officers of both battalions were asked to issue their own orders as they deemed fit.

The brigade was aware that the delay in launching an attack from the southern side posed a significant risk. The Haji Pir Pass had been under Indian control since 28 August

1965 and the absence of an established link-up from the southern side left the Indian Army vulnerable. The Pakistanis could encircle the pass and reclaim it through a counter-offensive. The stakes were high. Recognizing the urgency, 93 Brigade understood that further delay was not an option.

41

FIRST ATTACK ON RAJA POST, POK, 2–3 SEPTEMBER 1965

The Indian Army's attack from the Poonch side had been delayed by nine days, but finally, everything was in place and the troops were raring to go.

After the O group meeting, Lt Col N.N. Khanna and Lt Col R.B. Nair, the commanding officers of 2 Sikh and 3 Dogra Battalions, respectively, arrived at their designated Assembly Areas (AAs) on the border at around 2 p.m.

The soldiers of their battalions had already reached in the morning. The first action that both the commanding officers took after arriving was to issue their orders.

The scheduled time for 3 Dogra's attack on Raja was 9.30 p.m. on 2 September 1965, and after wiping out the enemy, their order was to take over the feature latest by midnight. Once they had declared their win on the communication net, 2 Sikh was to cross the Raja feature and approach Rani.

The FUP for 2 Sikh Battalion was on the northern slope of the Raja feature, and they were expected to immediately launch the attack on Rani from there. The time given to them to capture Rani was 10 a.m. on 3 September 1965.

Overall, it was a good plan, though a bit ambitious. In any case, 93 Brigade knew that more delay would endanger 1 Para, which had by now occupied the Haji Pir Pass, making it vulnerable to counter-attacks from the enemy from the south and the west. But once the Indians succeeded in establishing a link-up with 1 Para from the south side, it would not only definitively eliminate the possibility of an enemy attack from that direction, it would also make the redrawn Indian border impregnable to Pakistani attacks from the western side due to the bolstered Indian strength.

Shortly after sunset, 3 Dogra Battalion began its movement, with 2 Sikh following closely behind. Crossing Indian Post 405 on the CFL, 3 Dogra carefully approached the southern slope of Raja.

Along this slope, two distinct trees, positioned close to each other in a relatively flat area, were known as Bhai-Bhai. This marked the FUP for 3 Dogra before launching the attack.

Nearly 1000 Indian troops, equivalent to the fighting strength of two battalions, were quietly advancing towards Bhai-Bhai. They had eaten their final warm meal at the AAs, readied their weapons and, by midnight, they were optimistic about seizing the Raja post. Their plan extended to capturing the Rani post by morning.

Lt Col R.B. Nair was leading the troops. Beside him walked Maj. Greesh Chand Verma, the most senior company commander of the 3 Dogra Battalion.

Lt Col R.B. Nair said, 'Major Verma, once we reach the FUP, we need to launch the attack right away.'

'Okay, sir.'

'The enemy's artillery is quite strong. But we are relatively safe until we reach the FUP. What's their men and weapon status?'

'Sir, according to intelligence, there are 400 enemy troops at Raja and Rani. They have two 3.7-inch howitzers, one 25-pounder gun, two 81-inch mortars, eight Browning machine guns (BMGs) and other automatic weapons.'

'Roger.'

'But you are right, sir, they won't target us yet because so far out, they will only end up wasting their ammunition.'

'I hope so. But, considering the fact that the enemy has a huge pile-up of ammunition, they might commence engaging us any time now.'

They had barely moved 100 yards when the battalions came under heavy fire from Pakistani artillery. The Indians were quick to take cover and it slowed their forward movement. But, just as anticipated, the enemy fire was largely ineffective due to the long range.

To shield the troops, the Indians started bombarding the enemy positions at Raja and Rani using various artillery, including 3.7-inch howitzers, 25-pounders, 120 mm mortars and 5.5-inch machine guns, all at the same time.

Additionally, 3-inch mortars from 3 Rajputana Rifles, 3 Dogra and 2 Sikh were fired from Point 405. As a deceptive measure, other Indian picquets of 93 Brigade along the CFL also initiated firing at Raja and Rani.

As the bombs flew over them in the sky, the Indian soldiers kept moving forward.

Eventually, 3 Dogra reached Bhai-Bhai, their FUP, at 4 a.m., facing a delay of over six hours. The enemy had managed to impede the progress of the Indian forces, dealing a significant setback that the Indians were yet to realize.

Lt Col N.N. Khanna had ordered 2 Sikh Battalion to halt a little short of Bhai-Bhai. In the darkness, the Sikh soldiers waited as the Dogras launched their attack at around 4.30 a.m. Their war cry, '*Jwala Mata ki jai*', was heard at 5 a.m.

From their position, the soldiers of 2 Sikh heard intense firing and cries of men falling.

Lt Col N.N. Khanna had no idea how the fight was progressing. Everyone waited with bated breath, their eyes wide with anticipation and their weapons ready in their hands.

At 5.15 a.m., 2 Sikh received the victory signal from 3 Dogra. This was a very swift action by the Indians and Lt Col N.N. Khanna immediately ordered his Charlie and Delta Companies to move forward, cross Raja and attack Rani. These companies were led by Capt. Anup Dharni and Capt. Surjit Singh.

Before Lt Col N.N. Khanna could order Alpha and Bravo Companies to move ahead too, he was contacted by Capt. Anup Dharni on the radio, 'Sir, we are being targeted by machine gun fire from Raja.'

'How is that possible? The firing must be from behind them . . . from Rani.'

'Sir . . .' The CO could hear a lot of noise.

Capt. Anup Dharni came back on the line, 'Sir, we have lost one jawan. The firing is from Raja. Something is amiss.'

'Okay, Captain. Both companies take cover and hold your positions until further orders.'

'Roger and out.'

The CO turned towards the adjutant, Maj. Sukhinder Singh, and said, 'Contact 3 Dogra and check the latest status.'

'Okay, sir.'

Maj. Sukhinder Singh contacted the 2 i/c of 3 Dogra and realized that 3 Dogra had issued the victory signal without assessing the real situation.

The 2 i/c of 3 Dogra said, 'Looks like we made a mistake, sir. Our troops are yet to capture Raja.'

Maj. Sukhinder Singh immediately informed his CO, 'Sir, it appears there has been a communication gap. 3 Dogra is yet to conquer Raja.'

The CO immediately ordered his Charlie and Delta Companies back to their position short of Bhai-Bhai.

The events that followed were disappointing. Despite the Dogras' courageous efforts, they were unable to capture the heavily fortified enemy position at Raja, resulting in significant casualties for 3 Dogra.

Brig. Zora Singh, who was monitoring the situation live in the war room at Poonch headquarters, ordered the immediate withdrawal of both 3 Dogra and 2 Sikh to the AA.

3 Dogra and 2 Sikh Battalions moved back to the AA. The wounded soldiers of 3 Dogra were immediately provided medical attention, and no one was sure what would happen next.

A few hours later, the brigade commander directed the battalions to return to Poonch with the injured and fallen soldiers. All company and platoon commanders, along with the commanding officers of the battalions, were instructed to attend a conference the following morning.

Similar to the initial attacks launched from Uri by 1 Para on Sank and by 19 Punjab on Bedori Hill, the first attack from Poonch, led by 3 Dogra and 2 Sikh, also met with failure.

42

93 BRIGADE HEADQUARTERS,
POONCH, 4 SEPTEMBER 1965

By 9 a.m. on 4 September 1965, the officers and JCOs had assembled in the conference hall of the brigade headquarters in Poonch cantonment. Everyone was quiet and they were waiting for the brigade commander.

The brigade commander, in turn, was waiting outside on the porch for the arrival of Maj. Gen. Amreek Singh, the GOC. As soon as the brigade commander saw the major general's two-starred car approach the driveway, he came to attention.

The shining black Ambassador car came to a halt in the porch and a jawan smartly reached out to the door to open it. Maj. Gen. Amreek Singh stepped out.

Brig. Zora Singh saluted him and Maj. Gen. Amreek Singh reciprocated. The two officers then proceeded towards the conference hall.

As soon as Maj. Gen. Amreek Singh had finished responding to the greetings of the officers and JCOs in the conference hall, Maj. G.C. Verma started the presentation with the help of the sand model that lay before them.

'Sir, the artillery's attack on Raja yesterday had failed to damage the enemy materially or morally. My company had succeeded in reaching their wired boundary at Raja without much difficulty, but once we reached it, it was like walking into a wall of fire. The enemy has sited their guns very well on the fixed lines of our expected approach and there was no cover for our troops.'

The Maj. Gen. asked, 'Why did you make the false victory signal?'

The major looked at his CO, Lt Col Nair, and then continued, 'Sir, the victory signal was a mistake on our part, though unintended.'

'Continue.'

'Sir, as soon as we crossed the wired boundary, we were fired upon from both Raja and Rani. They had coordinated firing from a higher position. As predicted, the area beyond the boundary was also mined. Moving forward would have wiped out our entire battalion.'

'So, what's your recommendation? How do we capture Raja and Rani?'

'Sir, we need to plan our strategy differently. I don't think attacking them from the direction we tried yesterday is a good idea.'

There was pin-drop silence now. Brig. Zora Singh seemed upset with the explanation provided. His immediate boss was present in the conference hall and he was not sure if the reasons given were justification enough.

Maj. Gen. Amreek Singh noticed this and decided to take the lead, 'Major Verma, your battalion has done a tremendous job. We are proud of you. I understand the situation and accept your explanation. You may sit down now.'

Maj. G.C. Verma placed the wooden pointer down and took his seat.

Maj. Gen. Amreek Singh continued, 'What should we do next? Any bright ideas?'

There was an uncomfortable silence for a few seconds. After a minute, Lt Col N.N. Khanna cleared his throat to speak.

'Sir, give Raja to me. My boys of 2 Sikh will capture Raja. But before you approve, sir, I have a request to make.'

'Go ahead.'

'I need two days to conduct a reconnaissance of the whole area before I launch the attack.'

Maj. Gen. Amreek Singh looked at Brig. Zora Singh.

Brig. Zora Singh said, 'Sir, I recommend a change in ORBAT. Let 2 Sikh attack Raja and let 3 Dogra attack Rani. I also agree with Colonel Khanna regarding familiarization. We should delay the attack by two days so that a detailed recce can be carried out by the battalion.'

'Okay then, as GOC, I approve the attack on Raja by 2 Sikh and Rani by 3 Dogra. Best wishes, Colonel Khanna, Colonel Nair and everyone who's a part of this operation.'

43

93 BRIGADE HEADQUARTERS, POONCH, 4 SEPTEMBER 1965

Lt Col Narinder Nath Khanna was born in Larkana in Sindh province of undivided India on 20 May 1928. After completing his schooling in Pune and later in Delhi, he joined the National Defence Academy, from which he passed out at the age of nineteen. On 12 September 1948, he was commissioned into the Sikh regiment. Therefore, by September 1965, Lt Col Khanna had nearly seventeen years of experience in the army and he was thirty-seven years old.

It's a strange fact that the main architect of Operation Gibraltar, Pakistan's foreign minister, Zulfikar Ali Bhutto, was born in Larkana in the same year as Lt Col N.N. Khanna, i.e., in 1928. The next few days would show how Lt Col N.N. Khanna threw a spanner into the evil designs of Mr Bhutto and derailed his well-planned, though devious, Operation Gibraltar. For the moment, let's get back to the story.

On 4 September 1965, at around noon, Lt Col N.N. Khanna began addressing the troops of 2 Sikh Battalion, '*Mere bahadur jawanon,* GOC *ne hamein Raja ko* capture *karne ki zimmedaari di hai. Aap sab ne kal dekha tha ki dushman ki nafri kitni jyada hai aur uske paas kitna gola barood hai. Lekin hum Sikh hain, aur hum pe rab ki meher hai* (My brave Sikh soldiers, GOC has given us the responsibility of capturing Raja. You saw yesterday that the enemy is not just massing in large numbers, but they have a lot of weapons and ammunition too. We are all Sikhs here, and we have the blessings of God.'

One of the JCOs shouted, '*Jo bole so nihal . . .*'

Everyone shouted back, '*Sat sri akal* (one will be blessed eternally who says that God is the ultimate truth)!'

The collective shouting of the war cry at the top of their lungs by all the battalion's soldiers echoed in the Poonch cantonment and birds flew from the trees.

The CO continued, '*Lekin hamein poori taiyyari ke saath* attack *karna hoga.* Brigade commander *sahab ne hamein do din* recce *ke liye diye hain.* Recce *ke saath saath* Arty *wale dushman ki* guns *ki* ranging *bhi karenge. Hum 6 tareekh ko* attack *karenge. Main kal apne* orders issue *kar dunga. Koi sawaal?* (But we will have to attack with full preparations. Brigade commander has given us two full days to conduct a recce. The artillery team will range the enemy's guns in this time. We will attack the enemy on the sixth. I'll issue the orders tomorrow. Any questions?)'

The Sikh soldiers looked back at their CO, their jaws clenched, eyes unblinking and shoulders squared. Their silence was the proof of their focus.

It was now the time for the CO to shout the war cry, '*Jo bole so nihal . . .*'

The jawans shouted back in chorus, '*Sat sri akal!*'

After the address, the CO nominated Capt. Anup Dharni, the company commander of Charlie Company, and the battalion intelligence NCO, Hav. Ujagar Singh, to undertake night patrols and carry out a detailed reconnaissance.

He told them, 'This attack on Raja by 2 Sikh and on Rani by 3 Dogra will go on simultaneously. I want you two to take your patrols tonight and split up only when you think you have moved as close as possible to Raja. I'm planning an attack on Raja from two directions so that we can divide the enemy's frontage. But I will take a final call based on your feedback. Once you are back with on-ground information, we will decide about the directions of our attack and the most suitable location of our FUP. Clear?'

Both replied, 'Yes, sir.'

Then Capt. Anup Dharni asked, 'Sir, how deep do you want us to penetrate into enemy territory?'

'As much as possible. But don't cross the wired boundary as the area after that is likely to be mined. Take risks, but only calculated risks, okay? This is a do-or-die situation for us. Without us making forward movement, 1 Para soldiers are like sitting ducks in enemy territory. We don't have a moment to lose. Just two days of recce and we will go in with all we have.'

'Yes, sir.' They saluted and left.

44

RAJA FEATURE, POK (ACROSS CFL), 5 SEPTEMBER 1965

The reconnaissance patrols, under the command of Capt. Anup Dharni and Hav. Ujagar Singh, reached Post 405 on the Indian side of the CFL by 5 p.m. on 4 September 1965.

2 Lt Naubahar Chand, with his platoon equipped with RCL (recoilless) 57 mm guns, had already arrived and was awaiting orders to target enemy bunkers on Raja.

The initial action conducted by the reconnaissance patrols of 2 Sikh involved a visual inspection. The prominent features in the vicinity were clear to them: Raja stood directly in front, while on the left was the Rani feature situated in the deep, and on its right was Malta, a hillock lightly held by the enemy.

Capt. Anup Dharni focused his attention on the area between Raja and Malta. The terrain appeared to be a jungle on a gentle slope, hinting at a potential direction for one of their attacks.

Just after sunset, both patrols of 2 Sikh left the Indian Post 405 and crossed the CFL. The moon was in its first quarter, so they were relatively safe from detection at the enemy's Observation Posts (OPs) and Listening Posts (LPs). They moved stealthily and crossed the Bhai-Bhai feature at 1 a.m.

The reconnaissance patrols were well aware that the moon would set at 1.30 a.m., signalling the opportune moment for the real action to commence.

Once the moon vanished, plunging the area into complete darkness, they initiated their advance. After covering approximately 300 yards beyond Bhai-Bhai, where the ground began to incline towards the Raja feature, they decided to split up.

Capt. Anup Dharni moved towards the wooded area on the left, while Hav. Ujagar Singh moved towards the right. Capt. Dharni had barely gone 100 yards when he ran into trouble.

From Post 405, the area that had appeared to be rising gently was not only too thickly wooded, it was also naturally protected by a cliff. At one point, a dog at Raja started to bark. A couple of other dogs joined it.

Capt. Dharni and his patrol stopped in their tracks. That's when they heard the animated voices of the Pakistani soldiers from the top. They waited and just as expected, the enemy lobbed a few grenades in the darkness and fired a few random shots.

Finally, after spending a couple of hours in vain attempting to find a passage, the patrol decided it was time to return to the rendezvous position.

Hav. Ujagar Singh had a different experience. He found a track just below the ridge that rose towards the Raja feature. Using the shelter provided by the natural feature, he moved along with his patrol until they reached the wire perimeter of the enemy. They were now looking at Raja from the south-eastern side and it seemed well-protected. That's when they heard the grenades exploding and a few shots fired from Raja towards the south-western side. Though these sounds worried him, Hav. Ujagar Singh knew he could do nothing from here and hoped the other patrol would be safe.

From his position, Hav. Ujagar Singh decided to make a bold move. They were so close to the enemy territory that one slip-up and the enemy would learn of their presence.

He whispered to his soldiers, 'I want a volunteer to go forward and throw a stone. Let's find out how alert the enemy is and the exact location of their big guns.'

The next second, L/Nk Joginder Singh of Delta Company whispered, 'I volunteer, sir.'

As the patrol retreated 100 yards and sought cover, L/Nk Joginder Singh waited, aware of the significant risk he was taking. Spotting a large boulder, he approached it, selected a palm-sized stone and threw it with all his strength towards Raja.

Within three seconds, as he dived behind the boulder, the night sky erupted with a barrage of gunfire from Raja. The enemy was 100 per cent alert. Once more, the Indian soldiers recognized that they were facing trained soldiers of the Pakistan Army, not militia or semi-trained mercenaries.

After the guns fell silent, L/Nk Joginder Singh rejoined Hav. Ujagar Singh and the rest of the patrol. Carefully, the group made their way back to the rendezvous position, where

Capt. Anup Dharni had already arrived with his patrol. Together, they retraced their steps to the Indian Post 405 on the CFL and eventually returned to the Poonch cantonment just as dawn was breaking.

45.

93 BRIGADE HEADQUARTERS, POONCH, AND RAJA AND RANI FEATURES, POK, 5 SEPTEMBER 1965

As Capt. Anup Dharni and Hav. Ujagar Singh were conducting their recce in the darkest hours of 4 September 1965, there were other actions afoot in Poonch.

Lt Col N.N. Khanna was giving the final touches to his attack strategy in the afternoon with his O group when he received a call from Brig. Zora Singh.

'Good evening, sir.'

'Good evening, Colonel Khanna. There is a change in plan and we need to advance our attack by a day.'

'I beg your pardon, sir?'

'Yes, it means you need to attack tomorrow night.'

'Sir, but I'm yet to complete the recce. Our patrols are out there. After their return in the morning, we need to rehearse our movements.'

'I know, I know. But this is beyond me.'

'But, sir, our recce was approved by the GOC.'

'The order of advancement is not from the GOC. In fact, it goes all the way up to the army chief, and to tell you the truth, I have been made to understand, right up to the desk of the prime minister. We need to launch the attack as soon as we can.'

'Okay, sir.'

'I want both 2 Sikh and 3 Dogra to move tomorrow morning. The revised ORBAT should reach you in a few minutes. Please plan your orders and movements accordingly.'

'Okay, sir.'

As Lt Col N.N. Khanna put the phone down, his forehead was creased with worry.

Therefore, just before dawn, as Capt. Anup Dharni and Hav. Ujagar Singh were returning to the cantonment, they saw vehicles carrying the troops of 2 Sikh and 3 Dogra leave the main gates.

A few minutes later, Capt. Anup Dharni and Hav. Ujagar Singh entered to find Lt Col N.N. Khanna in his office.

After saluting, Capt. Anup Dharni asked, 'Sir, those—'

'—are our troops. And we need to leave soon too. Are you two ready to share all your findings with the O group?'

'Yes, sir,' said both.

The CO was on his feet. They followed him out. A few seconds later, they entered the conference room.

Over the next one hour, after the recce details had been shared, Lt Col N.N. Khanna finalized the plan. Once everyone understood their roles, the formal orders were issued.

As the commanding officer and his O group advanced towards Post 405, 2 Lt Naubahar Chand received the green light to target enemy bunkers on Raja and Rani. According to intelligence reports, the enemy bunkers at Raja were nearly impervious and the feature lacked the natural protection of trees or rocks. In contrast, Rani was concealed within a dense forest of coniferous trees.

On Raja, the enemy had meticulously constructed bunkers by covering them with closely packed tree trunks and filling them with layers of mud. A network of shoulder-high trenches intricately connected the bunkers to facilitate efficient movements. The defence strategy employed on Raja was textbook-perfect.

An additional challenge arose due to limited access to reliable maps. While the absence of photographs was already known to the Indian forces, the reliance on outdated pre-Independence maps posed a hindrance. This issue became critical as the Indian Army was tasked with making incursions into enemy territory, advancing northward with the objective of linking up with 1 Para and capturing enemy posts along the way.

There was another problem. Operationally, the Indians had decided not to involve their Air Force over enemy soil so far.

As 2 Sikh and 3 Dogra soldiers moved forward in the night, they were aware of the challenges ahead. Meanwhile, Indian artillery targeted enemy bunkers on Raja and Rani as the troops reached their AAs. Taking a moment to rest, they relieved their tired shoulders by removing their heavy packs and sat down in small groups.

46

ATTACK ON RANI POST, CFL, NORTH OF POONCH, 5 SEPTEMBER 1965

At 9 p.m., 3 Dogra started to move towards its FAA with 2 Sikh moving out after a few minutes and heading to its FAA.

As they were slowly moving ahead, something strange happened. One sepoy by the name of Jarnail Singh of Charlie Company of 2 Sikh started to sing loudly. Others asked him to stop singing, but that only caused him to increase the volume of his voice.

Jarnail Singh's eyes glowed with dilated irises, his movements were both jerky and forceful. Overwhelmed by unprecedented enthusiasm, this robust Sikh soldier, a seasoned basketball player, seemed to be propelled by an uncontrollable zeal. To him, the imminent prospect of battling for India, the Sikh regiment and the Indian Army superseded all else.

When Sep. Jarnail Singh didn't stop singing, ignoring the orders of his section commander and his platoon commander, the senior JCO of Charlie Company, Sub. Gurcharan Singh, met Capt. Anup Dharni and said, 'Sir, we need to leave Sepoy Jarnail at the FAA. He can take care of our equipment there. We can't take him any further.'

'Approved.' Capt. Dharni accepted the proposal. No one from Charlie Company at that time had any idea what Jarnail would do in the later stages of the battle.

* * *

Under the cover of darkness, 3 Dogra commenced its movement from the FAA at midnight. At approximately 1.30 a.m., as they progressed steadily, the distant sound of MMG firing reached their ears. It became evident that 2 Sikh's movement had been exposed. Though this was a psychological setback for the Dogras, they pressed on undeterred, reaching their FUP by 4 a.m., precisely in time for the planned attack.

Amid complete radio silence, 3 Dogra awaited a crucial message from 2 Sikh. However, as time ticked away, the anticipated signal failed to materialize. They had no idea what situation 2 Sikh was in.

Finally, at 5 a.m., the signal from 2 Sikh arrived. It revealed that despite their timely departure at 2.30 a.m., 2 Sikh had encountered navigational challenges, leading to a delayed arrival at their FUP, an hour behind the scheduled time.

At 5 minutes past 5 a.m., both battalions crossed the start line for their respective attacks—2 Sikhs on Raja feature and 3 Dogra on Rani feature.

The achievement of 3 Dogra was the execution of their approach to the FUP beneath the Rani feature. Their movement had gone undetected by both the observation posts of Raja and Rani.

This advantage stemmed from the unexpected decision to bypass Raja and directly target Rani, catching the enemy off guard. The conventional expectation was for any assault on Rani to follow a successful attack on Raja first. This unorthodox approach by 3 Dogra showcased their discipline and stealth.

The northern position of Rani, nestled in the depths beyond Raja, made it appear less susceptible to a direct frontal assault. The enemy, anticipating an attack through Raja, could reinforce Rani accordingly. However, 3 Dogra's decision to assail Rani from an uphill approach, rather than conforming to the anticipated gradual gradient of the land feature, added an element of surprise.

Despite the previous setback of failing to capture the Raja post two days ago, 3 Dogra was determined not to repeat their mistakes. According to intelligence reports, approximately 100 well-armed enemy soldiers were identified as manning the Rani post.

Significantly, the enemy troops held an elevated position and possessed an understanding of the area's topography. In contrast, the Indian forces found themselves at a disadvantage due to their lower elevation and lack of awareness of the terrain features.

Sunrise was at nine minutes past 6 a.m., but just after 5 a.m., the brave jawans of 3 Dogra Battalion, led by their officers and JCOs and shouting their war cry, '*Jwala Mata ki jai*', climbed the Rani feature from an unexpected direction and attacked the enemy post. The attack by all the four companies on Rani was audacious.

With the sky just showing a hint of dawn in the east, the intense fight raged on for nearly an hour. Every muscle in the jawans' bodies was taut with stress, every breath a testament to their unyielding determination. The ferocity of their movements, the speed and power behind each strike, and the sheer willpower driving them forward turned the battlefield into a spectacle of raw human endurance and skill. Though it lasted under an hour, the fight felt like an eternity, each minute packed with explosive energy.

Maj. Greesh Chand Verma and Capt. G.S. Bawa, the two company commanders who led from the front, were hit by enemy fire and were martyred. Sub. Bansi Lal and fourteen other soldiers lost their lives. In addition, three officers, two JCOs and sixty soldiers were wounded.

As the victorious Dogras reorganized their battalion atop the Rani post, thirty-nine Pakistani soldiers' bodies were recovered and five were taken POWs.

A search of the captured enemy post revealed that Rani was being defended by a company of 4 Azad Kashmir Battalion and a platoon of 5 Zhob Militia. It also had one section of Browning .30 mm MMG and one section of 81-mm mortar.

The enemy had left behind a significant number of arms, ammunition and food supplies. The most prized among the food supplies was the desi ghee, which the soldiers of 3 Dogra and 2 Sikh would relish for the next few weeks.

Maj. Verma, Nk Prem Singh and Sep. Sukh Ram were awarded Vir Chakras and Capt. Bawa and Sub. Bansi Lal were awarded Sena medals for their bravery in this battle.

47

ATTACK ON RAJA POST, CFL, NORTH OF POONCH, 5 SEPTEMBER 1965

The most prominent feature on the ridge, Raja, stood tall as the key position held by the enemy. As per the brigade's intelligence, it was guarded by a company of 4 Azad Kashmir Battalion and a platoon of militia (later identified as 5 Zhob Militia).

Additionally, the defensive set-up included three sections of Browning .30 MMG, one section of 81-mm mortar and a Heavy Machine Gun (HMG). Complicating matters further, the enemy was at an elevated position with a flat and vegetation-free top.

This meant that during the final infantry assault, Indian soldiers would have to traverse a significant distance in the open while the enemy remained shielded in their bunkers, capable of picking off targets at will.

Due to these reasons, 3 Dogra Battalion could not succeed two days earlier and the brigade commander had to call off the attack and revise the operation strategy.

As outlined in the preceding chapter, 2 Sikh departed from its FAA at 2.30 a.m., reaching its FUP at 5 a.m., an hour later than planned.

During their time at the FAA, vigilant Pakistani observation posts detected their movement around 1.30 a.m., engaging them with machine gun fire. However, the firing ceased after 2 a.m. The enemy recognized a significant development, demonstrating patience and likely conserving ammunition. The element of surprise was no longer a factor in the impending Indian attack.

Finally, at 5 a.m., as soon as 2 Sikh arrived at its FUP, Lt Col N.N. Khanna, the commanding officer of 2 Sikh, sent a message to 3 Dogra.

The moment had arrived. As per the battalion's strategy, Charlie Company, commanded by Capt. Anup Dharni, was tasked with securing the FUP first, taking a stationary position in the designated area.

Following this, Alpha Company, under the leadership of Capt. Jai Singh, would launch an attack to seize and take control of the left side of Raja post. Simultaneously, Bravo and Delta Companies, led by Maj. K.C. Kelly and Capt. Surjit Singh, were assigned to capture the right side. Once both flanks of the Raja post were under control, Charlie Company would advance and capture the Malta post held by the enemy.

In the initial steps beyond the start line, Bravo Company faced a barrage of enemy fire. Maj. Kelly, leading the company, was wounded and fell to the ground. Initially, assuming it was a stumble on a rock or a tree stump, he attempted to rise but failed. His jawans swiftly moved him to a secure position and examined his injury—a gunshot wound to the knee, rendering him unable to stand or walk. Recognizing his incapacity, Maj. Kelly made the decision to pass the command of Bravo Company to the next senior, Sub. Balwant Singh.

Meanwhile, the MMG and mortar sections worked tirelessly to suppress the enemy by continuously bombarding Raja, forcing them to keep their heads down.

Delta Company started moving a few minutes after Bravo Company. They were greeted with a volley of fire and had to find shelter as bullets zipped past them and bombs exploded around them.

The time now was 5.25 a.m. and the pre-dawn light had partially illuminated the surroundings. While this favoured the enemy, it spelt disaster for the Indian troops.

Observing the deadlock from the FAA, Lt Col Khanna grew concerned—there were only forty-five minutes left until sunrise. Taking decisive action, he moved forward with his protection section and joined Bravo Company a few minutes later, finding them positioned just behind the perimeter fence.

From his position, he gazed up at the imposing Raja post held by the enemy. It was the first time he had seen it with his own eyes, and the sheer magnitude of the natural obstacle against the sky revealed a reality that couldn't be fully grasped from the reconnaissance observations of his team or the outdated pre-Partition maps.

He turned to his right, witnessing the soldiers of Delta Company engaged in combat. Glancing to his left, he observed Alpha Company locked in fierce battle.

Before departing from the FUP, Lt Col Khanna had informed the artillery battery commander of his intention to lead the charge up the hill himself.

In contrast to the Sikh soldiers, who all wore turbans, the CO had a rolled-up balaclava on his head.

Stripping off his green and white jersey, he began waving it over his head, rallying his troops with words of encouragement. As the light improved rapidly, he became visible to the enemy, and the insignia on his shoulders made his identity clear.

Without a moment's hesitation, Lt Col Khanna sprang forward, urging everyone to join him in the swift assault. With determination, he hurled the wire aside and charged ahead. Closing in on one of the foremost enemy bunkers, he skilfully tossed a grenade into their position. In the middle of this daring act, a bullet struck him on his upper left arm.

Seeing the CO's fearless action, all troops crossed the wired perimeters. While the CO was lucky not to have stepped on any of the mines, a few soldiers were not that lucky. The legs of two were blown off and another was seriously injured. This charge, as would emerge later, would unnerve the enemy and become a stepping stone to the battalion's success. But there was a lot more to follow.

Despite Lt Col Khanna's courageous leadership, he recognized that the situation was not improving. The previous artillery barrage from Indian guns had proven ineffective, causing minimal damage to the enemy.

Assessing the circumstances, he made the strategic decision to withdraw his battalion and sought cover fire from the artillery battery commander to minimize casualties during the extraction. His future plan involved launching a re-attack after subjecting the enemy to a relentless bombardment from heavy Indian artillery.

While providing instructions to the artillery battery commander, Lt Col Khanna sustained a second hit, likely from a burst of bullets, possibly originating from the .30 mm MMG. He began bleeding profusely and the soldiers administered a field dressing to his wounds. They recognized the severity of his injuries and Lt Col Khanna was evacuated on a stretcher.

Lt Col Khanna, despite his injuries, managed to issue a poignant final order before falling unconscious: he insisted that no one should be informed about his incapacitation.

With a sense of duty ingrained in his last conscious moments, he prioritized the morale and focus of his troops, keeping the information about his critical condition veiled to maintain the steadfastness of the men in the battle.

In the confusion and the leadership vacuum caused by Lt Col Khanna's incapacitation, the responsibility of guiding the companies and platoons fell to the younger officers.

Amid this tumult, Capt. Anup Dharni, leading Charlie Company, previously held in reserve at the FUP, stepped forward to assess the dire situation. A quick evaluation of the ongoing stalemate led him to a decisive realization: Alpha, Bravo and Delta Companies were struggling to overcome the enemy. Recognizing the urgency, Capt. Dharni understood that he needed to take proactive measures to contribute to the unfolding battle.

Venturing beyond the right flank of Delta Company, Capt. Anup Dharni navigated around the Raja hill. Opting for an approach with a steep climb, he aimed to surprise the enemy and disrupt their entrenched positions.

Simultaneously, the battlefield witnessed numerous displays of individual courage. Infused with the spirit of the Sikh regiment's war cry, '*Jo bole so nihal, sat sri akal*', the soldiers advanced boldly, quelling enemy LMG posts, hurling grenades and unleashing fire from their personal weapons in a valiant effort to forge ahead.

Nk Chand Singh, a section commander in B Company, was deeply angered by the scene surrounding him and resolved to intervene. Renowned for his fearlessness and holding the title of javelin throw champion in the battalion, he embarked on a mission of action.

Following four successful grenade attacks on the enemy's bunkers, he pressed forward for the fifth assault. This time, his aim was the Pakistani MMG post that had been wreaking havoc since their arrival.

Charging across open terrain with enemy bullets whizzing past him, Nk Chand Singh displayed exceptional bravery. Recognizing the peril to their own soldier, the Indian battery commander wisely called off the firing on enemy positions. This decision was aimed at preventing any inadvertent harm to Nk Chand Singh as he continued his charge towards the Pakistani MMG post.

In a remarkable stroke of fortune, Nk Chand Singh reached the enemy's MMG post without sustaining any injuries. When in close proximity, he launched a grenade, causing the occupants to be stunned by the explosion and wounded by shrapnel.

Displaying extraordinary courage, he bayonetted the disoriented occupants. Having accomplished this feat, he returned to his section unscathed. Over the next few minutes, he led assaults on five additional enemy bunkers, all within plain sight of his company situated below.

Over time, the tide of the battle began to shift in India's favour. Charlie Company, having stealthily approached Raja post from the eastern flank, managed to arrive unnoticed by the enemy at this point. The adversaries, engrossed in countering the southern assault, were blindsided by the unexpected manoeuvre from the east.

Having successfully cleared the enemy bunkers, Capt. Anup Dharni led the charge and became the first to reach the Pakistani post headquarters on Raja. The once fortified bunkers were now devoid of enemy presence, with the lifeless bodies of Pakistani soldiers scattered in the aftermath of the fierce engagement.

Just a few steps behind the post headquarters, Capt. Dharni discovered the lifeless body of a Pakistani soldier lying face-down. Turning the fallen soldier over, he recognized him as the Pakistani captain who had been observed earlier, moving among bunkers, motivating his men.

A gunshot wound through the soldier's chest left Capt. Dharni puzzled. The oddity arose because the post headquarters was situated on the reverse slope, making it unclear how a bullet from the south, east or west directions could have been responsible for the fatal shot.

Perplexed, Capt. Dharni scanned the surroundings to unravel the mystery of the soldier's demise.

The lifeless bodies strewn across Raja post were clad either in khaki, the distinctive uniform of regular Pakistan Army officers, or salwar kameez, the attire worn by the militias.

When he scanned the scene more closely, Capt. Dharni's attention was drawn to a body clad in olive green, the uniform of the Indian Army. Closer inspection revealed the truth—it was Sep. Jarnail Singh.

The revelation left Capt. Dharni bewildered and grappling with questions. Had Sep. Jarnail Singh single-handedly taken down the post commander? Or had a simultaneous exchange claimed both their lives?

The circumstances were incomprehensible, especially considering that Sep. Jarnail Singh had been assigned the duty of guarding the equipment at the AA, far from the front line. Yet, here he was, having reached the enemy post ahead of the entire 500-strong battalion, a testament to his solo feat.

Later, the battalion would recommend Sep. Jarnail Singh for a Maha Vir Chakra, which would be denied to him.

In a triumphant but costly victory, the courageous 2 Sikh Battalion seized control of the formidable Raja post. The price paid for this achievement was steep—one officer, two JCOs and thirty-seven jawans laid down their lives, while three officers, three JCOs and ninety-six jawans sustained injuries. Tragically, Lt Col N.N. Khanna, the valiant leader, succumbed to his injuries during evacuation from the battlefield.

The soldiers who had been in close proximity to Lt Col Khanna maintained strict confidentiality regarding his demise, adhering to his last orders. In an act of unwavering dedication, they ensured that news of his passing did not leak to either their own battalion or to the enemy. Although posthumous, Lt Col Khanna's leadership had guided his brave battalion to victory, adding a poignant note to the pride of the triumph.

Lt Col N.N. Khanna was awarded the prestigious Maha Vir Chakra in recognition of his gallantry and leadership during the battle. Nk Chand Singh was honoured with a Vir Chakra for his outstanding bravery on the battlefield.

Maj. K.C. Kelly, 2 Lt Keshav Singh, Hav. Dalip Singh and Nk Sarjit Singh were acknowledged with Mentioned-in-Dispatches (M-in-D), recognizing their contributions and valour in the face of adversity.

Sadly, the Pakistani officer who had commanded the militia platoon (possibly 5 Zhob Militia) so gallantly must remain anonymous, for no one can remember his name. What is remembered is the letter from his fiancée found on his body—they were to have been married in two months' time.

The 4 Azad Kashmir company was commanded by Capt. M. Azam (later Maj.). Sub. Abdul Aziz of the company was awarded the Sitara-e-Jurat for this defence action at Raja—both survived the 1965 war.

—*Capt. Amarinder Singh and Lt Gen. Tajindar Shergill, PVSM,* The Monsoon War: Young Officers Reminisce—1965 India–Pakistan War

48

LINK-UP WITH 1 PARA, POK, 8–10 SEPTEMBER 1965

The battalions of the 68 Brigade by now had successfully captured the majority of the northern part of the Haji Pir bulge.

Simultaneously, the battalions of the 93 Brigade were advancing northwards along the Poonch–Uri axis. However, as previously mentioned, the attack from Poonch, known as Operation Faulad, experienced a delay of almost nine days, disrupting the planned link-up schedule by a few days.

Following the successful capture of the Rani post by 3 Dogra, the battalion proceeded with its advance towards Chand Tekri as ordered by the brigade headquarters in Poonch. However, the Pakistani troops at Chand Tekri were firmly entrenched, presenting a formidable challenge.

Buoyed by their recent victory at the Rani post, the Indian forces launched an aggressive assault in an attempt to dislodge the enemy. Despite making multiple efforts, the Indians encountered difficulty in overcoming the Pakistani forces holding their ground at Chand Tekri.

By that time, the Meghdoot force, led by Maj. Megh Singh, had successfully reached the south side of the Kahuta bridge. Over the preceding days, the Meghdoot force had effectively cleared numerous smaller enemy picquets situated to the east of the north-south axis.

Upon reaching Kahuta, their primary objective was to launch an assault on an enemy ammunition dump. However, upon their arrival, it was discovered that the enemy had already abandoned the dump, making a strategic retreat deeper into POK.

Recognizing the impasse at Chand Tekri, the Meghdoot force, determined to break the deadlock, executed a daring attack from the eastern flank. The element of surprise, combined with their unwavering resolve, caught the Pakistani forces off guard.

Overwhelmed by the sudden assault, the Pakistani troops could no longer maintain their stronghold and were compelled to retreat, yielding ground to the advancing Meghdoot force and 3 Dogra Battalion.

As 19 Punjab continued its advance from the northern side of Kahuta bridge along the Uri–Poonch Road, the battalion encountered a surprising revelation—the road, dating back to the pre-1947 era, was still surprisingly motorable in certain sections.

The steady progress of 19 Punjab along this historic route added an intriguing dimension to the unfolding developments in the Haji Pir region. Their advance was a testament to meticulous planning and determination, a steady march through challenging terrain that was steeped in both historical significance and strategic importance. The brigade headquarters watched closely as this battalion forged ahead, their movements a beacon of hope and strength. However, as they pressed on, a formidable obstacle emerged in their path: a ridge that loomed imposingly, effectively blocking the Indian Army's route.

On 9 September 1965, Lt Col Sampuran Singh, the commanding officer of 19 Punjab, undertook the mission of capturing this ridge to clear the path leading to Kahuta. This was no ordinary task; it required not just military acumen but also exceptional courage and resolve. Demonstrating extraordinary leadership, Lt Col Sampuran Singh orchestrated three determined attacks, each one a display of tactical brilliance and sheer tenacity. Under his command, 19 Punjab relentlessly pushed back the enemy forces, their spirit unbroken even in the face of fierce resistance. The ridge was finally taken, and the route to the Kahuta bridge was cleared, marking a significant milestone in their campaign.

In recognition of his exceptional bravery and leadership, Lt Col Sampuran Singh was honoured with the Maha Vir Chakra. This award marked his second gallantry recognition during the operations, a testament to his indomitable spirit and exemplary service. Just a few days earlier, he had been awarded the Vir Chakra for his role in the capture of Bedori peak, another strategic victory that underscored his tactical genius and fearless approach (see chapter 28). His dual decorations not only highlighted his personal heroism but also served as an inspiring symbol of the valour and dedication of 19 Punjab.

On the morning of 10 September, at 10 a.m., the historic link-up was successfully established between 19 Punjab (of

68 Brigade from Uri) and 3 Dogra (of 93 Brigade from Poonch), with the formidable Meghdoot force witnessing this crucial moment.

This momentous event marked the cutting off of the entire land mass known as the Haji Pir bulge, approximately 500 sq. km. The Indian Army had achieved complete control over this strategic territory.

With this, the Indian Air Force began to play a vital role, supporting the troops and facilitating operations.

Helicopters from the Indian Air Force touched down at a local school in Kahuta, serving as a makeshift helipad. The helicopters delivered essential supplies, including rations and medical provisions. Injured personnel were airlifted to either Poonch or Srinagar for urgent medical attention, ensuring evacuation and support for the front line forces.

Maj. Megh Singh's leadership during the operations earned him the prestigious Vir Chakra.

Keeping the promise he had made before operations began, Lt Gen. Harbaksh Singh personally bestowed the rank of lieutenant colonel upon Maj. Megh Singh on 16 September 1965. The ceremony took place in the presence of Lt Gen. Kashmir Singh Katoch, the corps commander of XV Corps.

This remarkable turn of events highlighted Maj. Megh Singh's transformation from a disillusioned officer who had contemplated retirement just months earlier, into a true hero.

His visionary approach of forming a specialized force comprising trusted and rigorously trained soldiers in the most challenging conditions proved to be instrumental in the success of the mission.

In the subsequent days, the Indian forces consolidated their hard-earned gains, marking the conclusion of both Operation Bakshi and Operation Faulad.

This achievement was a ringing triumph for the Indian military and dealt a blow to Pakistani forces. With the Haji Pir Pass under Indian control, the infiltrators found themselves trapped within the confines of Kashmir, devoid of any route back into Pakistan.

Those insurgents who chose to surrender their arms were taken POWs. However, those who persisted in hostilities against the Indian Army were met with decisive action.

Operation Gibraltar, initially conceived as a religious and 'liberation' movement, supported by a combination of military and militia elements and financed by the highest echelons of the Pakistani government, particularly the office of Field Marshal and President Mohammed Ayub Khan, ultimately suffered a resounding failure.

'Rumours about an impending operation were rife but the army had not shared the plans with other forces,' Air Marshal Nur Khan said. Sharing his memoirs with *Dawn* on the fortieth anniversary of the 1965 war, Air Marshal Khan said that he was the most disturbed man on the day, instead of feeling proud.

Air Marshal (retired) Asghar Khan, while handing over the command to Nur Khan, had not briefed him about any impending war because he was not aware of it himself. So, in order to double check, Nur Khan called on the then commander-in-chief, Gen. Musa Khan.

Under his searching questions Gen. Musa wilted and with a sheepish smile admitted that something was afoot. Nur Khan's immediate reaction was that this would mean war. But, Gen. Musa said he need not worry as, according to him. Indians would not retaliate. Then he directed a still highly sceptical Nur Khan to Lt Gen. Akhtar Hasan Malik, GOC Kashmir, the man in charge of 'Operation Gibraltar' for further details. The long and short of his discussion with Gen. Malik was, 'Don't worry, because the plan to send some eight lakh infiltrators inside the occupied territory to throw out the Indian troops with the help of the local population', was so designed that the Indians would not be able to retaliate and therefore the air force did not need to get into war-time mode.

A still incredulous Nur Khan was shocked when, on further inquiry, he found that except for a small coterie of top generals, very few in the armed forces knew about 'Operation Gibraltar'. He asked himself how good, intelligent and professional people like Musa and Malik could be so naive, so irresponsible.

For the air marshal, it was unbelievable. Even the then Lahore garrison commander had not been taken into confidence. And the governor of West Pakistan, Malik Amir Mohammad Khan of Kalabagh, did not know what was afoot and had gone to Murree for vacations.

—*Air Marshal Nur Khan (retd) in* Dawn, *Karachi,*
6 September 2004

AFTERWORD

As a young officer from the Signals' branch, entrusted with the responsibility of managing communications at 68 Brigade headquarters, Uri, Jammu and Kashmir, during the intense days of the Battle of Haji Pir, my role was far from the front line, yet integral to the success of the operations. At the heart of the complex web of information and orders, I found myself directly accountable to the astute Brig. Zorawar Chand Bakshi at brigade headquarters.

Being a signals officer afforded me a unique vantage point, granting me insight into every unfolding action during the Haji Pir capture and the subsequent endeavours to establish a vital link-up from the south. The significance of effective communication in the theatre of war cannot be overstated, and it was through the meticulous coordination of messages, updates and orders that the various elements of our forces functioned as a cohesive whole.

The narrative within these pages vividly captures the valour, the challenges and the strategic brilliance displayed by our armed forces during those critical days. From my position, I witnessed the ebb and flow of communication that seamlessly connected the participating units, allowing for a synchronized effort that ultimately led to the capture of Haji Pir.

Having been an eyewitness to the triumph of Haji Pir, I also had the opportunity to reach the captured heights soon after their fall. Being on the ground, I could witness first-hand some of the immediate actions taking place nearby, further cementing my appreciation for the coordinated efforts that contributed to this significant victory.

The resolute actions undertaken by the valiant 68 Brigade during the months of August and September in 1965 are still an enduring source of inspiration for every member of the Indian Army. The indomitable spirit and unwavering commitment displayed by these soldiers in the face of adversity continue to resonate through the annals of military history. Among the many triumphs achieved during this period, the capture of Haji Pir emerges as a beacon of shining glory within the Indian Armed Forces.

The significance of the Haji Pir operation goes beyond mere territorial gains; it encapsulates the epitome of strategic brilliance, tactical acumen and unyielding determination. This historic achievement not only showcased the exceptional valour of our forces but also served as a testament to the meticulous planning and flawless execution orchestrated by the 68 Brigade.

As we reflect upon these moments, it is imperative to extend a heartfelt salute to all those who played a pivotal role in this crucial battle. Their sacrifices, courage and steadfast commitment to the defence of our nation exemplify the very essence of the Indian Army's ethos. The legacy forged on the heights of Haji Pir continues to cast a profound influence, instilling a sense of pride and motivation in every individual donning the uniform.

In commemorating the triumph of Haji Pir, we honour the memory of those who fought bravely, ensuring that their legacy lives on as an eternal flame illuminating the path for future generations of warriors. May the tale of their valour inspire the Indian Army to reach greater heights and uphold the noble traditions set by these gallant soldiers.

The capture of Haji Pir marked a pivotal moment in our military campaign, but the significance extended beyond its strategic boundaries. The acquisition of additional key features by various battalions played an indispensable role in securing the entirety of the Haji Pir bulge, a testament to the comprehensive and well-coordinated efforts of our forces.

The names of these critical features resonate like echoes of sacrifice and triumph: Bedori, Bisali, Raja, Rani, Chand Tekri, Ring Contour, Sank, Gitian and the Kahuta bridge. These were not merely geographical locations; they were hard-fought battlegrounds, each demanding a toll in courage, determination and the ultimate sacrifice from our officers and jawans.

The battles for these features were fierce, involving uphill infantry assaults strategically complemented by artillery support. The daunting terrain and the formidable enemy resistance made each victory a testament to the grit and resilience of our armed forces. Behind the triumphs were stories of heroism etched with the blood and sweat of the brave men who faced adversity head-on.

It is essential to recognize that not every warrior who contributed to these victories received formal gallantry awards, but the absence of medals does not diminish the valour they displayed. Every soldier who fought in the relentless pursuit of securing the Haji Pir bulge exemplified unwavering bravery, unyielding commitment and a deep-rooted patriotism that transcended personal safety for the greater cause.

Let our heartfelt salute extend to every soldier, known and unknown, who played a role in the capture of the Haji Pir bulge. Their sacrifices, often unnoticed by the larger world, are forever etched in the annals of our military history, a testament to the collective heroism that defines the spirit of our armed forces.

Brigadier Shamsher Singh, AVSM (retd)
1 February 2024

ACKNOWLEDGEMENTS

I extend my gratitude to all who have supported, encouraged and patiently guided me throughout this journey. The individuals and organizations listed below have played pivotal roles in shaping this book and their contributions are appreciated. Please note that the names are listed in no particular order.

After conducting extensive research on the Haji Pir battle, I had embarked on a journey to the headquarters of 1 Para Battalion in Nahan, Himachal Pradesh, believing it to be the best starting point for my exploration. I express my appreciation to Colonel (Col) Rakesh Tokas, the commanding officer of 1 Para, and all the officers and jawans for guiding me through the co-located museum. The museum has captivating photographs of the operation, offering invaluable insights. A particular highlight of my visit was seeing the 9 mm carbine once used by Maj. Ranjit Singh

Dyal, prominently displayed in the officers' mess of 1 Para. Bearing the marks of Pakistani bullets, this carbine serves as a poignant reminder of Maj. Dyal's remarkable courage during the battle. I am honoured to include a photograph of this carbine in the book.

I express my gratitude to Brig. Arvinder Singh, the former company commander of Delta Company of 1 Para, which played a pivotal role in capturing the Haji Pir Pass. Despite sustaining a serious leg injury while leading his company (he was in hospital for four months and took two years to walk properly again), Brig. Arvinder Singh vividly recalls the battle's details to this day. I had the pleasure of meeting him at his residence in Noida (Delhi-NCR), where he generously shared the intricacies of the operation and his company's involvement. Additionally, my sincere thanks to Brig. Shamsher Singh, with whom I had a phone conversation initially when he was in Pune and finally met him at his residence in Noida. Serving as the sparrow (officer-in-charge of the 68 Brigade's signal company) throughout the battle, Brig. Shamsher Singh provided valuable insights that helped corroborate the information in this book. I'm also grateful to him for writing an afterword for this book.

I had the privilege of meeting Ms Parveen Dyal, daughter of Lt Gen. Ranjit Singh Dyal, in Panchkula, Haryana. I extend my heartfelt gratitude for her warm hospitality and for generously sharing valuable insights about her father. Additionally, she graciously opened her family album and shared family memorabilia, enriching my understanding of her father. Throughout our interaction, her husband, Jangveer Singh, provided unwavering support, for which I am equally thankful.

I extend my gratitude to Lt Gen. M.A. Gurbaxani, whom I had the privilege of meeting at his residence in Mumbai. Lt Gen. Gurbaxani, who served in the 4 Rajput Battalion and was wounded during the Haji Pir battle, provided invaluable insights. He directed me to Col Ranbir Singh, whom I had the pleasure of meeting during a visit to his house in Mohali, Punjab. Both Lt Gen. Gurbaxani and Col Ranbir Singh offered invaluable contributions that greatly aided in reconstructing the left claw of the pincer attack, shedding light on the initial setbacks and eventual success.

I am also thankful to Col Surjit Singh Sandhu, whom I met at his residence in Chandigarh. Col Sandhu, associated with the 6 Dogra Battalion that later joined the offensive under the 68 Brigade, played a crucial role in capturing the Gitian feature. His insights have been instrumental in enriching the narrative of the battle for the Haji Pir bulge.

I drove to Surjanwas village in Haryana to meet L/Hav. Umrao Singh's family, hoping to learn more about him since I couldn't find any information online except for the Vir Chakra citation.

Remarkably, upon inquiring about Umrao Singh's residence by name, the villagers promptly directed me to his house, even though Umrao Singh had made the ultimate sacrifice on 30 August 1965, in the battlefield. I extend my gratitude to L/Hav.'s Umrao Singh's son Karanbir Singh and grandson Hav. Ajit Singh (retd) for their warm hospitality and for sharing insightful details about this war hero. Following the meeting, they escorted me to the memorial dedicated to L/Hav. Umrao Singh, a poignant tribute built and maintained by the family in the village.

In Chandigarh, I had the privilege of meeting Col J.S. Bindra, who served as the adjutant of 1 Para as a captain during the pivotal Haji Pir attack in August 1965. His first-hand account has been invaluable, confirming much of the information I had gathered during my research. I am deeply grateful to him for his generous support.

I am also grateful to Rajeev Bakshi, son of the late Lt Gen. Zorawar Chand Bakshi, who served as the commander of 68 Brigade as a brigadier, for sharing insights about his father over the phone.

I extend my gratitude to Wing Commander M.A. Afraz (retd), the founder of Honour Point. It was during a chance meeting in Bengaluru that he reignited my interest in the Haji Pir battle. His mention of the battle sparked a connection within me as I recalled the Vir Chakra awardee, L/Hav. Umrao Singh, from a village neighbouring my maternal village. This pivotal moment marked the beginning of my journey towards researching and writing this book.

I extend my gratitude to Dr Ishwar Singh Yadav, who generously shared a wealth of news articles and documents related to this battle, collected over decades.

My sincere thanks to the librarian, in particular Vijendra Kumar Sharma, and the dedicated staff at the USI library in Delhi. I spent numerous days immersed in their extensive collection of books and periodicals, which enriched my research.

I express my gratitude to Sandeep Unnithan, a distinguished defence journalist and acclaimed author, for providing a glowing endorsement for the book. My gratitude is also due to Maj. Gen. Neeraj Bali and Maj. Gen. Paramjit Singh Sandhu for their endorsements.

Just as during the writing of my previous book, *The Battle of Rezang La*, my brother, Col (Dr) Andy Anil, has been my steadfast companion on every visit for this book. His unwavering support, encompassing emotional, technical (Army-related) and moral aspects, has played a crucial role in the creation of this book.

My mother has patiently listened to my narratives about the battle, offering encouragement with a gentle pat on my head. The love reflected in her eyes serves as a constant inspiration, motivating me to strive for excellence each day.

My heartfelt thanks extend to my loving wife, Seema, who stood by me as I navigated the challenges of time and resources while writing this book. Above all, my daughters, Liana and Mehal, serve as my psychological north stars, and the mere thought of them propels me to strive for improvement with each journey, such as this one.

Many thanks are also due to my family and close friends in India and abroad for their love and support over the years.

Finally, thank you, Milee Ashwarya at Penguin Random House India, for publishing this book, and Suhail Mathur of the Book Bakers for representing it. Additionally, thank you, the stellar team at PRHI, including Rachna, Ralph Rebello and Chandna Arora for their legal and editorial support.

GLOSSARY

1. **FAA (Forward Assembly Area):** A small area within an operational area or battlefield (usually in a sheltered location) where a military unit assembles and makes preparations for an attack before the final advance. This is usually outside the range of the enemy's artillery.
2. **FUP (Forming Up Place):** The last position occupied by the attacking soldiers before crossing the 'line of departure' or 'start line', sometimes also called the 'attack position'.
3. **CFL (Cease-Fire Line):** After the partition of India, present-day India and Pakistan contested the princely state of Jammu and Kashmir—India because of the ruler's accession to the country, and Pakistan by virtue of the state's Muslim-majority population. The First Kashmir War in 1947 lasted more than a year until a ceasefire was arranged through the United Nations' mediation. Both

sides agreed on a Cease-Fire Line. After the signing of the Shimla Agreement in July 1972 between India and Pakistan, the name CFL was changed to LoC (Line of Control), which is the term used today.

4. **GOC** (General Officer Commanding): The GOC of a division is a major general rank officer and is called GOC of Division.

5. **GOC-in-C** (General Officer Commanding-in-Chief): In the Indian Army's command structure, this is a senior lieutenant general rank officer who is also called an army commander.

6. **Cedar trees:** A type of coniferous tree in the plant family Pinaceae that is native to the mountains of the western Himalayas and the Mediterranean region. These trees can grow up to 60 metres high, though their average height is around 40 metres.

7. **Spur**: A spur is a lateral ridge or a piece of high ground that sticks out from the side of a hill or a mountain.

8. **Field Marshal**: A five-star rank in many armies across the world, field marshal or FM is the highest rank in the army, senior even to the chief of army staff, and is usually awarded on the basis of extraordinary military achievement. Only two officers in India have been promoted to the rank of field marshal—K.M. Cariappa and Sam Manekshaw. In Pakistan, only one officer has been promoted to the rank of Field Marshal, namely Mohammed Ayub Khan.

9. **Company**: A company is a military unit typically consisting of around 100–150 soldiers and usually commanded by a major or a captain. There are four companies in a battalion of the Indian Army and they are called Alpha, Bravo, Charlie and Delta.

10. **Corps**: In 1965, in the Indian Army, a corps typically had three divisions under its command and an artillery brigade, besides its core troops. A corps is commanded by an officer of the rank of lieutenant general.

11. **Command**: A command (or a unit) is an organizational entity in the Indian Army that is led by a military commander. Depending on its size, a command can be smaller or larger. For example, the command of a company is in the hands of an officer of the rank of major or captain, whereas, the command of a platoon is in the hands of a JCO (Junior Commissioned Officer). As a rule of thumb, the larger the command, the more senior would be the rank of its commander.

12. *Degchi*: A cooking vessel with a deep body and a large mouth. Originating in South Asia, a degchi is typically used for slow cooking and may or may not have a lid to cover its mouth.

13. **FFD (Forward Field Dressing)**: FFD is a type of bandage carried by soldiers in sealed waterproof pouches to keep it clean and dry, and it is used to dress wounds sustained during action. It typically consists of a large pad of absorbent cloth that is attached to the middle of a strip of thin fabric that can be tied or taped to the body.

14. **FOO (Forward Observation Officer)**: Because artillery is an indirect fire weapon system and cannons/howitzers/mortars are typically not able see their targets, which are often located miles away, an FOO serves as the 'eyes' of the guns by sending target locations and, if necessary, corrections to the fall of bombs by a radio set, so that gun crew can suitably alter elevation and range before firing subsequent rounds. The FOO moves and places himself

as close to the target as possible without being detected before the start of firing.

15. **25-pounder guns and bombs**: Designed in the 1930s by the United Kingdom, 25-pounder bombs were fired using field guns (howitzers), during World War II. The bomb weighs 11.5 kg and can travel up to a maximum range of 12 km. The Indian Army had used these till the 1971 war with Pakistan.

16. **Browning .30 mm MMG (Medium Machine Gun)**: A belt-fed automatic gun of medium weight that could fire 400–600 rounds per minute and had an effective range of around 1400 metres. Several variants were used during World War II and in other wars in the decades that followed.

17. **Portable radio set**: Battery-operated communication equipment that uses VHF/MF/HF frequency bands to transmit and receive verbal or non-verbal messages between units.

18. **Langar**: Langar is a common term used across various units in the Indian Army when referring to a cookhouse for troops, sometimes even when there is no building and the food is served in the open in the area adjacent to where it is cooked.

19. **Battalion**: In the Indian Army, a battalion is a military unit that consists of approximately 800 jawans and is commanded by an officer of the rank of a lieutenant colonel (now a colonel commands a battalion). It has three or four companies under it, each comprising 100 to 150 jawans and commanded by a captain or major.

20. **Adjutant**: A military officer who disseminates and coordinates the commanding officer's operational/administrative orders to the battalion.

21. **O group**: In the context of a battalion, O group stands for Order group and typically comprises the commanding officer, all company commanders, adjutant, intelligence officer, battalion quartermaster, subedar major, etc.

22. **NCO (Non-Commissioned Officer)**: Indian Army ranks from lance naik to havildar are collectively called NCO.

23. **Quartermaster**: An officer of the rank of captain or major who has charge of the logistic stores and ammunition of a unit.

24. **Infantry brigade**: In the Indian Army, an infantry brigade is commanded by a brigadier and consists of three infantry battalions along with supporting arms and services, viz. armoured squadron/troop, engineers company, artillery battery, signal company and EME (Electronics and Mechanical Engineers) workshop.

25. **Division**: An Indian Army division is headed by a general officer commanding (GOC) holding the rank of major general. It usually consists of 15,000 combat troops and 8000 support elements and can have three or more brigades under its command.

26. **FSMO Scale A or *bada pithu***: Field Service Marching Order (Pack 08/Scale A) is a large haversack that rests on the back of a soldier. It has a standard list of items including a small haversack, blanket, field dressing, rain cap, water bottle, mess tin, extra combat dress, etc., and weighs around 20 kg depending on the total items being carried, which are often mission-specific. There are two pouches in front that are hooked to the belt and are meant to store grenades and ammunition.

27. **Section**: A section is the smallest sub-unit of the Indian Army that can fight an independent battle. There are

three sections in a platoon and it comprises around ten personnel. The highest officer in a section is called a section commander and is usually an NCO.

28. **Platoon**: A platoon is an army unit that operates under a company and comprises around fifty personnel. In the Indian Army, there are three platoons under a company, each commanded by a JCO.

29. **Shakkarparas:** Sweet dough of refined wheat flour that has been cut into rectangles around 2–3 inches in length, an inch in width and a quarter of an inch in thickness, and deep-fried. This high-energy snack can last for a couple of weeks in almost any weather.

30. **CQMH (Company Quartermaster Havildar):** CQMH is a senior NCO who has charge of the company's logistics, administration, weapons and ammunition, etc.

31. **Mortar**: A mortar is a lightweight and portable weapon that consists of a smooth/rifled metal tube fixed to a base plate (to spread out the recoil) with a lightweight bipod mount and a sight for direction and ranging. Mortars launch explosive shells (bombs) in high-arching ballistic trajectories and are typically used as indirect fire weapons for close fire support. The bombs are loaded directly from the top of the tube.

32. **Sitrep**: Situation reports or sitreps are periodic reports exchanged between military formations usually along the chain of hierarchy, from lower to higher, and follow a predetermined time and format.

33. **Very pistol**: A large-bore handgun that is also called a 'signal pistol' or 'flare gun'. It is used to fire illuminating flares that act as a warning, distress or success signal.

34. **Batman**: Now called 'buddy' in the Indian Army, a batman is a soldier who assists an officer with preparation of his uniforms, conveying messages and, if required, any other role, like driving the officer's vehicle, acting as the officer's bodyguard and other miscellaneous work that the officer orders him to do.

35. **Company Havildar Major (CHM)**: NCO in charge of a company. His charter of duties includes all operational and administrative roles, including the discipline of the company. The CHM closely monitors the conversations of the troops and keeps an eye on them.

36. **Magneto telephone**: A hand-cranked telephone that uses permanent magnets to produce alternating current from a rotating armature that causes telephones on the same line to ring.

37. **2 i/c**: The second-in-command of any formation is called a 2 i/c. In case of a battalion, the 2 i/c is junior only to the commanding officer of the battalion and functions as the commanding officer in case of the absence of the appointed commanding officer.

38. **SEATO**: SEATO, formed in 1955, aimed at a collective defence in South-east Asia against communist expansion. Despite hindrances and internal conflicts limiting its military effectiveness, SEATO's cultural and educational initiatives had lasting impacts in the region. It was dissolved on 30 June 1977 due to waning interest and withdrawals.

39. **CENTO**: Originally named the Middle East Treaty Organization (METO) and later known as the Baghdad Pact, the Central Treaty Organization (CENTO) emerged as a Cold War military alliance. Established

on 24 February 1955, it included Iran, Iraq, Pakistan, Turkey and the United Kingdom. The alliance was dissolved on 16 March 1979.

40. **SMR (Sand Model Room)**: A special room where sand models are used for military planning and wargaming. It's like a small-scale map used in training for military actions.

41. **Barakhana**: Barakhana is a tradition in the Indian Army in which all ranks come together to dine as one cohesive family. This gathering is designed to cultivate a sense of brotherhood and camaraderie, and instil the confidence that, when it comes to the shared objectives of the unit, everyone stands united.

42. **ORBAT (Order of Battle)**: When an armed force participates in a military action or a campaign, the ORBAT states the hierarchical structure, manpower, disposition of soldiers and the equipment status of the units and formations of the participating armed organization.

43. **D-Day**: The scheduled date when the armed unit is slated to attack.

44. **H-Hour**: The scheduled time when the armed unit is slated to attack.

45. **Nullah (or nallah)**: The term 'nullah' typically refers to a small, narrow and usually dry watercourse or streambed, especially one that is found in arid or semi-arid regions. In South Asian countries, particularly in India, Pakistan and Bangladesh, the term is commonly used to describe a seasonal stream or drainage channel that may only carry water during the monsoon season or heavy rainfall. The word 'nullah' is derived from Hindi and Urdu.

46. **3.7-inch mountain howitzers**: A 3.7-inch howitzer is a wheeled mountain gun that was used during World Wars I and II by the British and Commonwealth armies. The Indian Army had used it in the 1965 and 1971 wars against Pakistan. Its maximum range is around 5400 metres.

47. **Zhob Militia**: The Zhob Militia is a paramilitary regiment within the Frontier Corps, a civil armed force situated in Baluchistan, Pakistan. It holds the distinction of being one of the oldest paramilitary forces in the region. Operating under the jurisdiction of the Frontier Corps, the militia is led by officers seconded from the Pakistan Army.

48. **81-mm mortar**: An 81-mm mortar is a medium-weight weapon used by infantry units for long-range indirect fire support. It can be employed by light infantry, air assault and airborne units, covering the entire front of a battalion's zone of influence.

BIBLIOGRAPHY

1. P.C. Katoch, 'Battle of Haji Pir: The Army's Glory in 1965', https://idsa.in/system/files/jds/jds_9_3_2015_BattleofHajiPir_0.pdf.
2. 'Indo-Pakistani War of 1965', https://en.wikipedia.org/wiki/Indo-Pakistani_War_of_1965.
3. 'Battle of Haji Pir Pass (1965)', https://en.wikipedia.org/wiki/Battle_of_Haji_Pir_Pass_(1965).
4. Bharat Rakshak: Official War History, 1965, History Division, Ministry of Defence, Government of India, http://www.bharat-rakshak.com/ARMY/history/1965war/275-war-history-1965.html.
5. M. Ilyas Khan, 'Operation Gibraltar: The Pakistani Troops Who Infiltrated Kashmir to Start a Rebellion', BBC News, https://www.bbc.com/news/world-asia-34136689.

6. 'Capture of Haji Pir Pass', produced by Films Division, Govt. of India, https://www.youtube.com/watch?v=rP6vb8GS4LE.

7. 'India Brigadier: "I lost seven of my boys in the battle",' BBC News, https://www.bbc.com/news/av/world-asia-india-33882459.

8. Diaries of Field Marshal Mohammed Ayub Khan (President of Pakistan), 1966–1972 (Karachi: Oxford University Press).

9. Lt Gen. (retired) Kamal Matinuddin, 'Operation Gibraltar revisited', *The News International*, Pakistan, https://web.archive.org/web/20070930015348/http://www.thenews.com.pk/editorial_detail.asp?id=22817.

10. Maj. Gen. Afsir Karim (retd), 'The 1965 War: Lessons Yet to Be Learnt', Rediff.com, https://in.rediff.com/news/2005/sep/19war.htm.

11. Dr Ahmed Faruqui, 'Remembering 6th of September 1965', https://web.archive.org/web/20070930165129/http://www.pakistanlink.com/Opinion/2004/Sept04/17/05.html.

12. Cyril Almeida, 'Gibraltar, Grand Slam and War', *Dawn*, https://www.dawn.com/news/1203708.

13. 'Air Marshal Nur Khan (retd) reminisces '65 war', *Dawn* – https://www.dawn.com/news/155474/nur-khan-reminisces.

14. Col Bhaskar Sarkar, 'Battle of Haji Pir', *Indian Defence Review*, http://www.indiandefencereview.com/spotlights/battle-of-hajipir-pass-1965/.

15. Dinesh Kumar, 'Return of Haji Pir Still Haunts Us', *Tribune*, https://www.tribuneindia.com/news/archive/comment/return-of-haji-pir-still-haunts-us-287239.

16. Rachna Bisht, *1965: Stories from the Second Indo–Pakistan War* (Penguin Books India).

17. Scott Gates, *Limited War in South Asia: From Decolonization to Recent Times* (Routledge).

18. Archana Masih, 'Why Did India Give Back the Haji Pir Pass to Pakistan?', https://www.rediff.com/news/special/why-did-india-give-back-the-haji-pir-pass-to-pakistan/20150923.htm.

19. Capt. Amarinder Singh, 'General Harbaksh Singh: Modern India's Greatest Soldier', https://www.sikhphilosophy.net/threads/general-harbaksh-singh-modern-indias-greatest-soldier.30304/.

20. Maj. Agha Humayun Amin, OPERATION GRAND SLAM (extract), https://www.brownpundits.com/2018/02/17/operation-grand-slam-1965-war/.

21. Gen. Akhtar Hussain Malik's Letter to His Brother Gen. Abdul Ali Malik, https://www.brownpundits.com/2019/08/19/letter-of-general-akhtar-malik-re-grand-slam/.

22. Raghav Gakhar, 'Battle of Haji Pir Pass—When Indian Special Forces Conquered the Impossible', https://defencelover.in/battle-haji-pir-pass-indian-special-forces/.

23. 'India's Original Surgical Strike: How the Haji Pir Pass Was Captured in 1965', ThePrint, https://theprint.in/pageturner/excerpt/indias-original-surgical-strike-how-the-haji-pir-pass-was-captured-in-1965/128551/.

24. Arjun Subramaniam, *India's Wars: A Military History, 1947–1971* (HarperCollins India).

25. G.D. Bakshi, *India Pakistan War 1965*.

26. P.V.S. Jagan Mohan and Samir Chopra, *The India–Pakistan Air War of 1965* (Manohar Publishers).

27. Lt Gen. Harbaksh Singh, *War Despatches: Indo–Pak Conflict 1965* (Lancer International).

28. Victoria Schofield, *Kashmir in Conflict: India, Pakistan and the Unending War* (Bloomsbury India).

29. Capt. Amarinder Singh and Lt Gen. Tajindar Shergill, *The Monsoon War: Young Officers Reminisce—1965 India–Pakistan War* (Lustre).

30. Lt Gen. Harbaksh Singh, *In the Line of Duty: A Soldier Remembers* (Lancer).

31. Shiv Kunal Verma, *1965: A Western Sunrise* (Aleph).

32. C. Christine Fair, *Fighting to the End: The Pakistan Army's Way of War* (Oxford).

33. Ayesha Siddiqa, *Military Inc.: Inside Pakistan's Military Economy* (Penguin India).

34. Iqbal Chand Malhotra and Maroof Raza, *Kashmir's Untold Story* (Bloomsbury India).

35. Shekhar Gupta, '1965 India-Pakistan War, who won or lost & why it was a war of mutual incompetence' | ep 259, https://youtu.be/wcNN4OA13Ok.

36. '1965 India–Pakistan War: How Indian Army Fought after Losing to China in 1962', https://www.youtube.com/watch?v=hKj4nRgpsQY&t=14s.

37. Interview with Ms Parveen K. Dyal, daughter of Lt Gen. Ranjit Singh Dyal, Maha Vir Chakra awardee for 1965 war, when he was a major.

38. Manu Pubby, 'India–Pak War: The Man Who Captured the Hajipir Pass', *Indian Express*, 21 February 2012, https://indianexpress.com/article/news-archive/web/indiapak-war-the-man-who-captured-the-hajipir-pass/.

39. Josy Joseph, 'Haji Pir Conqueror Says Handing It Back to Pak Was a Mistake ', Rediff news, 22 December 2002, https://www.rediff.com/news/2002/dec/21haji.htm.

40. Maj. Gen. H.S. Kler, 'The Capture of Haji Pir Pass', 30 October 2015, https://salute.co.in/the-capture-of-hajipir-pass/.

41. 1965 India–Pakistan War Commemoration Day, Honourpoint, https://www.honourpoint.in/indo-pak-war-1965/.

42. Rohit Agarwal, *Brave Men of War: Tales of Valour 1965* (Bloomsbury, 2015).

43. Nitin A. Gokhale, *1965 Turning the Tide: How India Won the War* (Bloomsbury, 2015).

44. Maj. Gen. Dhruv C. Katoch, *Honour Redeemed and Other Stories from the 1965 Indo–Pak War* (Bloomsbury India).

45. R.D Pradhan, *1965 War: The Inside Story, Defence Minister Y.B. Chavan's Diary of India–Pakistan War* (Atlantic Publishers).

46. Farooq Naseem Bajwa, *From Kutch to Tashkent, the India–Pakistan War of 1965* (C. Hurst & Co. Publishers Ltd: United Kingdom).

47. Maj. Gen. Lachhman Singh, *Missed Opportunities, Indo–Pak War 1965.*

48. The War Decorated India Trust, Vir Chakra (VrC) Awardee: Hav. Umrao, VrC, http://twdi.in/node/4733.

49. 'Capture of Haji Pir Pass, ADGPI – India Army', https://youtu.be/6eG7JRNCUes.

50. Col Awadhesh Kumar, 'Saga of Major Arvinder Singh, Who Led His Company to Victory on Hajipir Pass', https://www.indianpolitics.co.in/28-august-1965-saga-

of-major-arvinder-singh-who-led-his-company-to-victory-on-hajipir-pass/.

51. Indian Army Heroes – Battle of Hajipir Pass (part 1), https://www.youtube.com/watch?v=sy6zSSl6LcM.

52. Indian Army Heroes – Battle of Hajipir Pass (part 2), https://www.youtube.com/watch?v=VwJzYLlYrlg.

53. 'Capturing the Crucial Hajipir Pass', *Tribune*, https://cc.bingj.com/cache.aspx?q=col+prabhjinder+singh+hajipir&d=4916299035314718&mkt=en-IN&setlang=en-US&w=Uaaj7CCP1j67rJjcdgaSvaee7iSWfThp.

54. Maj. Gen. Raj Mehta, 'Militarily Won; Diplomatically Lost: The Haji Pir Saga', https://archive.claws.in/images/journals_doc/1734396434_Militarilywondiplomaticallylost.pdf.

55. K.D. Maini, 'Haji Pir, 9 am, 28 August 1965. Here is what happened next', *Dispatch*: https://www.thedispatch.in/haji-pir-9am-28-aug-1965-here-is-what-happened-next/.

56. Lt Col N.N. Khanna, 'The Citation for the Maha Vir Chakra', Honourpoint, https://www.honourpoint.in/profile/lt-col-narindra-nath-khanna-mvc/.

57. 'Stories of Magical Saints Keep up the Spirits of Villagers along the Line of Control', https://thewire.in/society/line-of-control-villages-poonch-jammu-and-kashmir.

58. Lt Gen. H.S. Panag, 'Winning the Raja Post from Pakistan', https://www.newslaundry.com/2016/07/08/winning-the-raja-post-from-pakistan.

59. Maj. Gen. P.K. Chakravorty, '1965 War – Pakistan's Strategic Blunder', https://indianarmy.nic.in/writereaddata/documents/Articles1965/PKChakravorty230915.pdf.

60. 'Gallant Commander Who Led by Example', *Hindustan Times*, https://www.hindustantimes.com/chandigarh/

gallant-commander-who-led-by-example/story-CusmU
PkybtieD4glXRMZGM.html.

61. 'The Rann of Kutch Arbitration', Cambridge University
Press, 28 March 2017, https://www.cambridge.org/
core/journals/american-journal-of-international-
law/article/abs/rann-of-kutch-arbitration/
F7969E80C0F9E51D47FC7E4F94B2D32C.

62. The War Decorated India and Trust, Citation of Brig.
Sampuran Singh, http://twdi.in/node/2155.

63. Maj. Gen. P.J.S. Sandhu (retd), '1965 Indo-Pak War –
A Critical Appraisal', USI (India), https://usiofindia.org/
publication/usi-journal/1965-indo-pak-war-a-critical-
appraisal/.

64. 'Dogra Regiment', Wikipedia, https://en.wikipedia.org/
wiki/Dogra_Regiment.

65. Lt Col Narindra Nath Khanna, MVC, Honour Point,
https://www.honourpoint.in/profile/lt-col-narindra-
nath-khanna-mvc/#:~:text=Lt%20Col%20Narindra%2
0Nath%20Khanna%20was%20a%20committed,
courage%2C%20unwavering%20leadership%20
and%20supreme%20sacrifice.%20Profile%20
Maintenance.

66. Maj. Gen. Sheru Thapliyal, 'Return of Haji Pir Pass in
1965 – Myth and the Reality', *Indian Defence Review*,
https://www.indiandefencereview.com/spotlights/
return-of-haji-pir-pass-in-1965-myth-and-the-reality/.

67. Raju Mansukhani, '1965 War: Infiltration in J&K by
Pakistan, Stories of Courage and Resilience', *Financial
Express*, https://www.financialexpress.com/business/
defence-1965-war-infiltration-in-jk-by-pakistan-stories-
of-courage-and-resilience-3205403/.

256

Bibliography

68. Tariq Bhat, 'Explained: How Militants Take Advantage
of Pir Panjal's Topography and Demography', *Week*,
https://www.theweek.in/news/india/2023/12/30/
explained-how-militants-take-advantage-pir-panjal-
topography-demography.html.

69. Deexa Khanduri, 'Remembering the 1965 Indo–
Pakistan War', Sputnik India, https://sputniknews.
in/20230923/remembering-the-1965-indo-pakistan-
war--4357760.html.

70. 'Central Treaty Organization', Wikipedia, https://
en.wikipedia.org/wiki/Central_Treaty_Organization.

71. 'Southeast Asia Treaty Organization', Wikipedia,
https://en.wikipedia.org/wiki/Southeast_Asia_Treaty_
Organization.

72. 'India-Pak War of 1965: Indian Army's Bhimber Gali
Brigade remembers Capt. Chander N Singh', Indian
Sentinels, https://www.indiasentinels.com/army/india-
pak-war-of-1965-indian-armys-bhimber-gali-brigade-
remembers-capt-chander-n-singh-4509.

73. Mentioned-in-Dispatches: The Capture of the Haji-
Pir Pass, Medium, https://der-wille.medium.com/
mention-in-dispatches-the-capture-of-the-haji-pir-pass-
36df29aca860.

74. 'Presentation on Haji Pir and Tangail', United Service
Institute, https://www.youtube.com/watch?v=P78mBFX
ZJ6A&t=1033s.

75. Interview with Rajeev Bakshi, son of Lt Gen. Zorawar
Chand Bakshi, over the phone.

76. Interview with Brig. Shamsher Singh, 68 Brigade, in
Noida.

77. Interview with Brig. Arvinder Singh of 1 Para (Delta Company) Battalion in Noida.
78. Interview with Lt Gen. M.A. Gurbaxani of 4 Rajput Battalion in Mumbai.
79. Interview with Col Ranbir Singh of 4 Rajput Battalion in Mohali, Punjab.
80. Interview with Col Surjit Singh Sandhu of 6 Dogra Battalion in Chandigarh.
81. Interview with Col J.S. Bindra of 1 Para Battalion in Chandigarh.
82. Interview with Col Rakesh Tokas, commanding officer, 1 Para Battalion in Nahan, Himachal Pradesh.
83. Interview with son and grandson of L/Hav. Umrao Singh, Delta Company, 1 Para Battalion in Surjanwas, district Mahendragarh, Haryana.

Scan QR code to access the
Penguin Random House India website